Praise for Mark David Gerson's Memoirs

Acts of Surrender
Dialogues with the Divine
Pilgrimage: A Fool's Journey
A Lifetime of Miracles (coming soon)

A dynamic read for the creative spirit within each of us. Positive inspiration at its best.
HANK BRUCE – AUTHOR OF "PEACE BEYOND ALL FEAR: A TRIBUTE TO JOHN DENVER'S VISION"

An absolute must for all fans of this immensely talented and generous writer.
PAOLA RIZZATO – GLASGOW, UK

A compelling journey of rare faith and courage. Insightful, poignant, inspiring!
NANCY EDELSTEIN – AUTHOR OF "YOUR PATH TO ONENESS"

A masterful work from one of today's masters.
JOAN CERIO – AUTHOR OF "HEARTWIRED TO HEAVEN"

An emotionally raw testament to the power of spiritual faith. A must-read!
ESTELLE BLACKBURN – AUTHOR OF "BROKEN LIVES"

I feel as if Mark David wrote this book just for me. Each page contains wisdom I need to hear. What a gift this book is.
KAREN HELENE WALKER – AUTHOR OF "THE WISHING STEPS"

I don't know anyone who has risked more, given up more, to be a writer.
WILLIAM REICHARD – AUTHOR OF "THIS ALBUM FULL OF ANGLES"

More from Mark David Gerson

FICTION

The MoonQuest, The StarQuest, The SunQuest

The Bard of Bryn Doon

The Lost Horse of Bryn Doon (coming soon)

The Sorcerer of Bryn Doon (coming soon)

Sara's Year

After Sara's Year

The Emmeline Papers

SELF-HELP & PERSONAL GROWTH

The Way of the Fool: How to Stop Worrying About Life and Start Living It

The Way of the Imperfect Fool: How to Bust the Addiction to Perfection That's Stifling Your Success

The Way of the Abundant Fool: How to Bust Free of "Not Enough" and Break Free into Prosperity

The Way of the Creative Fool: How to Bust Through Your Blocks and Unleash Your Full Creative Potential

The Book of Messages: Writings Inspired by Melchizedek

FOR WRITERS & ASPIRING WRITERS

The Voice of the Muse: Answering the Call to Write

The Voice of the Muse Companion: Guided Meditations for Writers

From Memory to Memoir: Writing the Stories of Your Life

Organic Screenwriting: Writing for Film, Naturally

Birthing Your Book...Even If You Don't Know What It's About

The Heartful Art of Revision: An Intuitive Guide to Editing

Writer's Block Unblocked: Seven Surefire Ways to Free Up Your Writing and Creative Flow

Time to Write

Write with Ease

Free Your Characters, Free Your Story

Write to Heal

Journal from the Heart

Write in the Flow!

PILGRIMAGE

A Fool's Journey

MARK DAVID GERSON

PILGRIMAGE: A FOOL'S JOURNEY

Copyright © 2021 Mark David Gerson
All rights reserved

No part of this book may be reproduced, stored in a retrieval system or transmitted by any means, electronic, mechanical, photocopying, recording or otherwise, without written permission from the author, except for the inclusion of brief quotations in critical reviews and certain other noncommercial uses permitted by copyright law.

And no part of this book may be used or reproduced in any manner for the purpose of training artificial intelligence technologies or systems.

First Edition

Published by MDG Media International
www.mdgmediainternational.com

ISBN: 978-1-950189-29-8 (paperback)
ISBN: 978-1-950189-30-4 (ebook)

Cover Image by Mark David Gerson: Day #7 – Back-back road between Helena and Billings, MT

Author Photo: Day #3 – iPhone selfie of Mark David Gerson and Kyri by the Columbia River's Wanapum Dam in Central Washington

More of Mark David Gerson's photography
www.markdavidgerson.photos

More information
www.markdavidgerson.com

> *Only those who risk going too far
> can possibly find out how far they can go.*
> T.S. ELIOT

> *As to me I know of nothing else but miracles.*
> WALT WHITMAN

> *Our life on Earth, this life, and the thousands we may have undergone before — perhaps they are part of but a single pilgrimage that we had in mind when we set out from some other home, somewhere else, long ago.*
> DAVID LEVITAN

In memory of Eve Hunter, who has taken the ultimate Fool's Journey.

Contents

Foreword	9
May 2019	17
June 2019	35
July 2019	101
August 2019	191
Afterword	305
The Music of "Pilgrimage"	313
Gratitude	317

Foreword

Dive into the unexpected, dance into the chaos.
The Way of the Imperfect Fool

Every day's surrender to these pages reminds me that what I'm writing about is now, not then.
Acts of Surrender: A Writer's Memoir

Three months before I launched the pilgrimage chronicled in these pages, I wrote a catch-up chapter to fill in the five-year gap between the first edition of my *Acts of Surrender* memoir and the new one I was preparing to release. As I revisited the giant leap of faith that had taken me from Albuquerque to Portland a year earlier — "among my most daring, and frightening, leaps into the unknown," I wrote — I couldn't know that I was on the cusp of a leap that would prove even more daring, and decidedly more terrifying.

Portland had gifted me with much, including Kyri, my first canine companion in two decades. I loved the city's urban vibe, its coffee culture and, a treat after so many years in the desert, its lush greenery. I even loved its gray, drizzly winters, which felt gentle and nurturing in a way the harsh Southwest sun never had. What Portland failed to provide, unfortunately, were the resources to sustain me there.

It wasn't the first time the financial rug had been pulled out from under me in the wake of a major life change. Twenty years earlier, within days of having moved to Hawaii, the independent, MLM-type income I had been counting on to support me there collapsed.

Something similar occurred not long after I moved to Portland. A first-installment payout for one of my screenplays, which was to have cushioned my early months in the city, disintegrated as only film-industry projects can. Within fifteen months, I had drained my savings and maxed out my credit. The countdown to an eviction notice soon began, and it became quickly apparent that not only could I not afford to move, I could not afford to stay in Portland.

If you have read any of my nonfiction or attended any of my

workshops, you will know that I rarely make decisions based on logic or conventional wisdom (which may be conventional, but is rarely wise). Instead, I do my best to surrender to a higher wisdom.

To be clear, that "higher wisdom" does not derive from some white-bearded, white-robed gentleman commanding the universe from some celestial perch. It is, as I put it in *Acts of Surrender*, "an infinite indwelling presence that is simultaneously my wisest aspect and the ineffable universality that is the sum of all that is."

I could call it God, divine intelligence, infinite mind, higher self, intuition or, when it comes to my writing, my Muse. I could call it Spirit or the Universe. I could call it Dan or Diane or the Great Pumpkin. The name doesn't matter. Whatever I might call it would be little more than an arbitrary label for a spirit and energy that lies beyond my mind's still-limited capacity to encompass…a spirit and energy I recognize to be wiser than the human me.

It was that higher wisdom that directed me to Portland and Hawaii, as well as to each of the many other places I have lived since my mid-thirties. It has written my nearly two dozen books and half-dozen screenplays and taken the lead in my hundreds of workshops and coaching sessions. It has governed all my major life decisions and many of the minor ones. And it has guided all my travels, including my four open-ended road odysseys — the ones I entered into willingly and joyfully and those, like the one you will read about here, that I entered into reluctantly and fearfully.

Reluctantly and fearfully is how I watched April 2019 melt into May as I prayed for the financial miracle that would keep me going. "I'm working on it," I would text my Portland landlord whenever he asked about my overdue rent. And every few hours I would go for a walk (I do my best meditating on foot) and try to access my higher wisdom for guidance…not always graciously: Too often, I would ask, "What the fuck am I supposed to do?" And more often than satisfied me, the only answer I would intuit was, "Stay the course."

I was living in Toronto in 1997 when I found myself nominally homeless. Then, it wasn't for financial reasons. It was because I couldn't find acceptable accommodation that would take Roxy, my cocker spaniel. I tell the story in greater detail in *Acts of Surrender* but, in brief, I spent ten days tapping my inner resources for a solution to my housing crisis — first from my tent in a provincial park, then from a series of hotels and motels. Finally, when I was ready to burst with frustration, a metaphoric lightbulb flashed on over my head, like I used to see in comic strips as a kid. In that instant of absolute clarity, I knew what I was to do: I would shut down my Toronto life, pack Roxy and my remaining possessions into my Dodge Caravan and head west. By then, I was too grateful to have been given *any* direction to be either reluctant or afraid.

When, two weeks into May 2019, I had my Portland "lightbulb moment," I was too frightened to be grateful: For the seventh time in twenty-two years, I was to divest myself of most everything I owned, and for the third time I was to stuff what was left in my car and take off for parts unknown. In 1997, I'd had savings. In 2004, I'd had the proceeds from selling off my household and an active sound-energy healing practice that I could continue from the road. In 2019, I had minimal moving-sale proceeds (the condo I rented was mostly furnished), no reliable income other than Social Security and a shitload of debt. Of course, I was terrified.

When I set out on that first pilgrimage in 1997, there wasn't much of a public internet, so my journey was largely private. Even contact with friends was minimal; cell phones were expensive and coverage outside major cities was spotty. And if the worldwide web was more prevalent by the time I set out on my second, the social media phenomenon was in its infancy and opportunities for publicly chronicling that journey were limited. By the time I left Portland in mid-2019, however, most of the developed world was cell-connected, online all the time and Facebook-centered...as was I. For this journey, I would share my travels through words and photos on Facebook, in my newsletter and on my blog.

My early posts were hopeful, focused more on my travels than on my feelings. Besides, I figured I had enough cash and credit to keep me going for a couple of weeks. I had to believe that something significant would shift for me before then.

But as days turned into weeks and weeks into months, I grew more despairing. Many mornings, I didn't know how I would muster the emotional strength to crawl out of bed and face another day of random, seemingly pointless wanderings. Yet, thanks to Kyri, who needed walking and feeding, I always did. And thanks to the endless succession of miracles that somehow kept me afloat, I always got back into the car to discover where it would carry me that day.

I passed through more than a dozen US states, some multiple times, during the ninety-three days of my pilgrimage. I passed through many more states of mind, all of which found their way into my writings, both public and private.

Some years back, at another time when nothing in my world made sense, my friend Sander urged me to chill for the rest of the day. That morning, I had taken what to that point was my most daring leap of faith ever, and he felt I needed a break. Here's how I tell it in *Acts of Surrender*.

"No," I responded, without thinking. "I think I'll go to Starbucks to write."

Sander argued with me, tried to convince me not to work.

"You don't understand," I countered. "Writing is the only thing that makes sense." *Then, to my surprise, I burst into tears.*

On this journey, too, writing was the only way I knew to make sense of an intuited call and series of experiences that made little sense to my conscious mind, let alone to many of my online acquaintances.

So, I wrote...minimally at first, then with increasing frequency and fervor. All those writings, public and private, are included here — uncensored and, apart from edits to add context and clarity, fill in gaps and remove redundancy, unaltered.

My fantasy novel *The MoonQuest* opens with the protagonist as an old man, pressed by the dreamwalker Na'an to fix the youthful journey that was his MoonQuest on parchment. Reluctant to revisit that time, he resists.

When it came to this book, I felt a similar reluctance, if for different reasons. In the end, though, the reasons mattered less than the ultimate surrender, both Toshar's and mine.

"The shadows will tell me the story," Toshar says as the light cast by his flickering taper dances against the night-darkened wall, "and I will write what I see. I will write until my fingers and beard are black with ink. I will write until the story is told. Only then will I be free to continue my journey."

I will do the same. As much as I would prefer to leave that slice of my past in the past, Na'an is right. By stepping back into that time from the perspective of today, I will not only gain insight into then, I will better understand now. Only then will I be free to continue *my* journey.

May 2019

It's not about what I want.
It's about what life wants from me.
And it looks like life has spoken.
The Emmeline Papers

The darkest path is the one with the most light.
And the most hopeless path is the most hopeful.
Trust that when the way seems blocked.
The StarQuest

"The Plan"

Wednesday, May 15
PORTLAND, OREGON

PREDAWN

Yesterday, after days of reassuring my landlord that "I'm working on it," it looked as though my time here might finally be up.

"Any updates?" he texted me. "I'm going to be forced to start the eviction notice if something doesn't happen very soon. I don't want to do it, but I won't have a choice."

"I understand," I replied. "Please give me until the end of the week before you take any action."

As I hit "send," I still had no idea what to do. Then, when I woke up about an hour ago, I did. I reached for my phone, opened the Notes app and jotted this down.

THE PLAN

Once I finish the Q'ntana upgrades[1] (don't ask me why I'm bothering), which should be today or tomorrow, I'll use the building's online bulletin board to sell as much stuff as I can. I don't think I'll be coming back to Portland once I leave, so nothing is going into storage. Whatever won't fit in the Prius will be donated or trashed. Then, I'll step out as the Fool does (big surprise), with all I own in my somewhat larger bindle.

---

[1]. A few months earlier, I had started a fourth story in my *Q'ntana* fantasy series, now rechristened *The Legend of Q'ntana* because I couldn't have a *Q'ntana Trilogy* with more than three stories. I had redesigned the existing books' covers and was now in the final stages of making the necessary adjustments to their copyright and other pages before uploading the updated book files to the relevant platforms.

What about Kyri? I don't want to re-home him, but is it practical for him to come?

Wait. If I really am stepping out as the Fool, it makes sense for him to come. Every tarot deck I've ever seen shows the Fool with a small dog. I guess it's up to him. If he finds himself a new home like Roxy did[2], I'll have to deal with it.

When the time comes to leave — I'm aiming for Tuesday, May 28, my sixteen-month anniversary in Portland — I'll take off in the car for parts unknown. Heading east on I-84 along the Columbia feels right, but that could change.

Hopefully, between whatever I score from the sale and whatever credit I'm able to stretch out, I can manage for maybe two weeks. Beyond that…? No idea…about lots of things…

- What do I keep and what do I let go of…in terms of everything, specifically my current recurring commitments? Things like Kyri's pet insurance, my Adobe Creative Cloud subscription, Netflix, my QuickBooks Online, etc.
- What do I do about my website? It renews at the end of the month, and it ain't cheap.
- Do I try to let some of my credit cards go? If so, which?
- Do I spring for camping gear? Camping would be cheaper than hotels/motels, but I doubt my back could take it anymore. It sure wasn't happy last time…and that was more than ten years ago on Mount Shasta.
- Where the hell do I go from I-84? I feel a bit of a pull toward the Atlantic and back to Nova Scotia[3]; that's probably nothing more than false nostalgia.

---

2. When I was moving to Hawaii, I knew Roxy couldn't come. Not only could I not afford the quarantine, I was certain that a dog as social as she was wouldn't do well locked away for a month. Thanks to a serendipitous encounter that was as heartbreaking for me as it was a relief, she found her own new home.

3. I lived in Nova Scotia for fourteen months in 1994-95; that's where I wrote most of the first two drafts of *The MoonQuest*.

This may be the purest Fool's journey I've ever undertaken. I'm not thrilled about it, but it's the "rightest-feeling" thing to show up, at a time when *something* needed to show up. I guess it'll either work and lead to a rebirth, or it will be my final journey. So I'll reach out to the landlord today, get the ball rolling and...

Going Public

Saturday, May 18
PORTLAND, OREGON

LATE EVENING

This is what I posted on my blog and sent out as a newsletter once I had finalized everything with my landlord.

"Portal land," my friend Sander jokingly remarked back in late 2017 when I told him I was moving to Portland. As it turned out, it was no joke.

Given that a portal is something you pass through as you move from one place or space to another, not a place you stay in, perhaps I should have paid closer attention to the notion of Portland as a portal when I moved here sixteen months ago expecting to stay indefinitely.

You see, I'll be leaving town on or around May 28. Likely for good.

As happened with my move from Toronto to rural Nova Scotia twenty-five years ago (and many times since), Portland turned out to be a sort of halfway house between an old chapter of my life and an as-yet unwritten new one.

Of course, I couldn't have known that when I moved here, at least not consciously. If I had, I couldn't have made the choices and decisions that sparked the growth (and growing pains) I have experienced here. It's likely no accident that I wrote my two *Way of the Fool* books here. And it's no accident that I launched my time here with a "Way of the Fool" talk at the New Thought Center for Spiritual Living in Lake Oswego and capped it this past Saturday with a "Way of the Fool" workshop at the New Renaissance Bookshop.

"If I were to choose an archetype to describe my life's journey,"

I wrote in my *Acts of Surrender* memoir long before there were *Way of the Fool* books, "it would be the Fool, a tarot character often pictured stepping off a cliff into the unknown."

If nothing else, my time in Portland has pushed me harder than at any other time in my life to more fully embrace that archetype… to more fully surrender to it…to more fully embody it.

Step #10 in my book *The Way of the Fool: How to Stop Worrying About Life and Start Living It…in 12½ Super-Simple Steps* is "Embrace the Mystery." Step #11 is "Embrace the Magic."

I will have to embrace the mystery and the magic when I drive out of Portland in ten days. That's because, in quintessential Fool-like fashion and not for the first time in my life, I will be leaving with no idea where I'm heading, where (or when) I'll land or how I'll finance the journey. Like the Fool, I will be leaving with my little dog, with minimal possessions (whatever fits into my Prius) and with as much faith and courage as I can muster.

I'm leaning toward driving east along the Columbia River. But whether I follow the river for a day before veering off in another direction — perhaps toward Bend, a place of magic and miracle when I passed through in 1997 — or all the way up into Canada, I cannot now know. Step #2 in *The Way of the Fool* is "Be In the Moment," so such decisions will likely come only as they're needed. After all, it was an in-the-moment decision like that that brought me into the United States twenty-two years ago, and that turned out pretty good.

All I know for certain is that when I pull out of the parking garage here for the last time in a few days, my car will determine where I'm going. That's the Way of the Fool.

"His may be a leap of faith," *Acts of Surrender* continues, "but it's never blind faith. For [the Fool] knows that even as he trades the certainty of solid ground for the mysteries of the void, the infinite wisdom of his infinite mind will guide him forward. This knowingness frees him to surrender again and again. And again. Not without resistance and not without fear, but in the conviction that resistance is futile, fear cannot stop him and meaning is always present, even when it is invisible."

I had lots of resistance and lots of fear in the uncertain weeks leading up to my moment of clarity a few days ago. Yet I knew I would surrender in the end. I always do.

"There will be more acts of surrender after this one," *Acts of Surrender* concludes. "There always are. Each one will push me harder than the last. Each one will nudge me closer to my essential truth. Each one will require a greater leap of faith. And through each, I will continue to trust in the story. Whether it's the story I'm writing or the story I'm living, it always knows best."

Day 1

Tuesday, May 28
Cascade Locks, Oregon

AFTERNOON

It was a stressful morning, not least because not everything that I hoped would fit into my Prius did, resulting in some panicky last-minute triage. I'd expected to hit the road earlier, but it was nearly eleven when I finally dropped the keys and fob onto the kitchen counter, took one last look at the home I was leaving behind, rode the elevator down to the garage, and started up my jam-packed car.

As I turned onto Kearney, then made my way along Lovejoy toward the Broadway Bridge, I watched the Pearl District chapter of my Portland life disappear behind me: the Safeway where I did much of my grocery shopping...my favorite cafes...the streetcars... the lanes and sidewalks where I walked Kyri most days...

I didn't cry. I was too numb to cry. Nor was I scared. I was too numb for that, too. All I wanted was to complete my two final errands, get out of Portland and leave behind the pain I couldn't bring myself to feel.

After making a stop at Comcast to return my router and at the Eddie Bauer Outlet store at the edge of town to buy a cooler, I rejoined eastbound I-84 and, within minutes, Portland was behind me.

I didn't look back.

Goldendale, Washington
EVENING

A natural land bridge once dammed the Columbia River near today's Cascade Locks, my first stop after leaving Portland. Although no one knows how long it took, the Columbia eventually broke through, freeing the river to once again flow unimpeded.

Today's Bridge of the Gods, which spans the Columbia at Cascade Locks, got its name from a Klickitats legend in which the chief of all gods fashioned a land bridge — a "bridge of the gods" — to link his rival sons who had settled on opposite shores. The bridge is said to have collapsed into the river during a battle between the feuding brothers.

Whatever natural disasters created then destroyed the original land bridge all those centuries ago, the metaphor of the power of flow smashing through a giant blockage felt important to acknowledge this afternoon with a return visit to the modern bridge.

My first time there was in 2006, in the midst of another road odyssey. The second was just shy of a year ago on a day trip from Portland. This third time was significant for more than the notion of breakthrough. This time for the first time, I drove across the bridge…out of Oregon.

As I continued east along the Washington side of the Columbia, I tried to leave all thoughts of my old life behind. And now, as I sit up in bed in my Goldendale motel room on this first night of my new life, I do my best not to worry about what that new life might look like.

Day 3

Thursday, May 30
GINKGO PETRIFIED FOREST STATE PARK, WASHINGTON

AFTERNOON

Passing through Washington's Ginkgo Petrified Forest State Park, I'm struck by the perfect metaphor of this place. I'm not petrified as in fossilized or immobilized. I *am* petrified, at least in moments, about this journey and what lies ahead.

So far, my only "inner guidance" has been to surrender to my intuition and trust it to lead me from moment-to-moment. Right now, it's pushing me toward the Gateway Arch in St. Louis. I don't feel any urgency to get there by a certain date, but I do feel an urgency to get there.

Meantime, I'm to trust that if I listen to the voice of my higher wisdom and follow where it leads me, I will be taken care of.

That has always proven true in the past, even if the means and manner of that "care" have often felt less than optimal. Still, it's harder to trust this time. And scarier. That's because the stakes are the highest they have ever been: I'm homeless with no apparent means of support, and I'm called on this Fool's journey that, barely forty-eight hours out, already feels more foolish than Fool-ish.

Yet it is only when the stakes are high that trust is required. How many ways I have written that in my books? How many ways have I spoken it to clients and in workshops? I can hate that it's true; it changes nothing. It *is* true. As Toshar is told in *The MoonQuest*, "You either trust or you do not. There is no halfway in between." Annoyingly, that maxim also shows up in *The StarQuest* and *The SunQuest*.

I may be petrified in moments, but I can't let my fear get in the way. I have to trust. I have to keep trusting...even if I don't think I can...even if I don't think I know how. That's the only way I will make it through this, whatever it is that "this" is.

That's what I say this afternoon in the Petrified Forest. I hope I am able to say it wherever I am tonight and tomorrow and the day after that...and for however long this goes on.

Day 4

Friday, May 31
PULLMAN, WASHINGTON

EVENING

I couldn't know, when I wrote my first *Way of the Fool* book last year in Portland, that I would be called to live its precepts more fully than I could ever have imagined. Yet here I am, much like the Fool on the classic tarot card, taking one leap of faith after the next as I travel the US (and maybe into Canada) with my little dog and with all I own stuffed into my bindle, which in my case is my Prius.

On this open-ended journey, I have no fixed destination and often know only in the moment where to go next. (Step #2 in *The Way of the Fool* is "Be In the Moment." Step #7 is "Take Risks," #9 is "Don't Give Up" and #10 is "Embrace the Mystery.")

Did I move to Portland so I could write the two *Fool* books that would ultimately push me out of Portland and onto this journey? Were those two *Fool* books my instruction manual for this pilgrimage? Maybe. Step #4 in *The Way of the Imperfect Fool* is "Trust the Journey"; #12½ is "See the Perfection in All Things."

What I know with absolute certainty, now that I'm four days into my travels, is that this is the highest path for me at this time, which eases but doesn't eliminate my apprehension and calls on more reserves of faith and courage than some days I believe I possess. What I also know with equal certainty is that, somehow, I have always been supported in every intuitive choice I have made and that I have never been let down when I have acted from my deepest heart. Even in my moments of most acute anxiety, I must acknowledge that.

Earlier today, one of my longtime Facebook friends, a deeply spiritual woman whose intuitive sensings I have always respected, responded to one of these "Fool's Journey" posts by encouraging me to enable people to support me financially through donations. To be honest, I was reluctant.

It has never been easy for me to ask for help or to accept it when offered. I probably inherited that independent streak from my mother, who saw it as a survival mechanism. A single, working mom at a time when they were rare — certainly in our circle of family and friends — she hung on to that self-sufficient attitude long after she no longer needed it, at least not financially. Watching cancer strip her of her independence along with her health was heartbreaking. But it helped me better appreciate the value of interdependence. Even so, when I read this morning's suggestion that I help the universe support me by putting out a call for donations, it was hard not to feel "less than," undeserving and a failure.

Could I ask for help? Could I ask for *financial* help? If I were to do it, could I do it in a way that wasn't disempowering, that didn't come from a place of lack? I thought back to the comments left on my posts in recent days and to the many people who have told me how touched and inspired they are by this Fool's Journey I have undertaken. Not only have I found such feedback to be deeply gratifying — particularly as, at the outset, I was too embarrassed by my predicament to want to share my day-to-day experiences of it — it showed me that this could be a fair "energy exchange": financial support in exchange for inspirational support.

Still, I hesitated. Was the notion of an energy exchange a bogus rationalization? Some people were bound to see it that way. Could I open myself to those criticisms? Could I let myself be that vulnerable?

I thought about it all day and, in the end, I couldn't not. Whether in my writing or my teaching, I have always endeavored to be open about my feelings and to encourage others to do likewise. The call to be vulnerable shows up, either directly or indirectly, in all my books, fiction and nonfiction. Perhaps it's best expressed in *From Memory to Memoir: Writing the Stories of Your Life*, where "Be

Vulnerable" is my "Rule"[4] #3 for memoir-writing: "Your vulnerability is a profound and powerful gift," I write. "It gives your readers permission to be vulnerable in their own lives."

Although sharing my emotional journey on the road *and* asking for help leave me feeling vulnerable in ways that make me profoundly uncomfortable, I can't teach what I don't practice. Given that, I will gratefully and humbly accept any donations you are moved to make to support me on this Fool's Journey. Whether or not you choose to support me financially, I am deeply grateful for all your blessings and good wishes. They help sustain me in my moments of doubt, which usually kick in around four in the morning and, too often, don't let me get back to sleep.

---

4. The word "rule" is in quotation marks because the first rule in all my books on writing is, "There are no rules."

June 2019

Trust your knowingness. Trust your calling.
Trust the journey.

*Dialogues with the Divine:
Encounters with My Wisest Self*

It is best not to know too much too soon. It is best to know only that the story continues and to follow where it takes you.

The SunQuest

Day 5

Saturday, June 1
MISSOULA, MONTANA

EVENING

Missoula and I have changed radically and grown dramatically in the twenty-two years since I was last here. Between those changes and my faulty memory, I have failed to locate any of the landmarks from my first visit, which took place about halfway through my 1997 road odyssey.

Back then, I was here for a week, long enough to witness the most breathtaking sunset I had ever seen, to meet a remarkable collection of like-spirited people through the local metaphysical bookstore and to become a Reiki master, which paved the way for so much that would follow in later years.

This time, I'm here only for the night. Yet even if I can't play spiritual tourist to my history, it's good to be back in the energy of a place that holds so many joyful and powerful memories.

Tomorrow, I head for Helena, retracing my steps from that 1997 journey, but in reverse. Last time, I was traveling from the East and drove through Wyoming's Bighorn Mountains before stopping in Helena on my way to Missoula. Now, I'm coming from the West. So it's Helena tomorrow, then the Bighorn Mountains.

There are a handful of spots in this country where I have had profound spiritual, metaphysical and/or transformational experiences, repeatedly. I'm unlikely to get back to all of them on this journey, given that several are in Hawaii. But I'm hoping to return to a particular one high up in the Bighorn Mountains. Each time I find myself in the area, I'm never certain I will be able to locate my "spot"…because I never remember its name or its precise location. Somehow, though, it always finds me. I'm counting on it being no different this time. Given the nature of this journey, I could use a potent spiritual, metaphysical and/or transformational experience right about now.

Day 7

Monday, June 3
Helena, Montana

MORNING

After writing, my next creative passion is photography. In fact, I was taking pictures with my Kodak Instamatic, and my Brownie prior to that, long before my Muse wore down my resistance to becoming a writer. I have always loved interpreting my world through the lens of a camera and sharing the resulting vision with others. That's one of the reasons why I have been posting so many photos on these travels. If I'm honest, though, snapping pics of what I'm seeing is often easier than writing about what I'm feeling.

This morning, for example, I woke up in full-on (not Fool-on) panic. Would I manifest the resources needed to keep going, or would I run out in the middle of some godforsaken nowhere? And what was I thinking, taking off like this with practically nothing? Where would I end up? How could I land anywhere with no "startup" funds?

It didn't help that while I was organizing some of my photos last night, I happened on those from my 2018 move from Albuquerque to Portland. I was scared then, too. But I was excited about my new life in Oregon and hopeful about all the ways it might play out. Yet here I was, barely eighteen months later, pushed out the other side of the Portland "portal" without a clue as to what awaits me, or where.

As I've mentioned here previously, *The Way of the Fool* covers all those human anxieties and more. To recap, largely for my benefit...

Step #2 is "Be In the Moment." *Am I okay today? Yes? Then there's nothing to worry about.*

Step #10 is "Embrace the Mystery." *It's okay to not know.*

Step #11 is "Embrace the Magic." *Miracles can show up in any moment. In fact, they're already present in each moment if we open our eyes, hearts and minds to see them.*

All the other steps in both *Way of the Fool* books also apply. The bottom line is that every word I have ever written and every precept I have ever taught as teacher and coach — and not only to writers — supports every aspect of this journey I have undertaken. So how can I do anything but surrender to it? After all, my memoir is titled *Acts of Surrender*.

Now, as I pack up for another day on this Fool's Journey, with no idea which road will call me or where it will take me, I am forced to remember all I have been, done and written (Step #12 is "Remember Who You Are") and to remember as well that whenever I have let go (Step #6) and followed my heart (Step #3) I have always been embraced and supported. Why would this journey be any different?

I wasn't going to share my morning panic publicly until I remembered *The Way of the Fool*'s Step #5 ("Be Vulnerable"). As I wrote here on Friday, by sharing our vulnerability we give others the courage to be vulnerable as well. I hope that one of my gifts to you in chronicling this journey is the permission it gives you to share *your* stories, vulnerably and from your heart. For, in the end, so much of what I'm about, through all I write and teach, is helping others to share their stories.

May your journey today be as wondrous as I now know mine will turn out to be…as it already is.

Day 8

Tuesday, June 4
BILLINGS, MONTANA

MORNING

It's the first day of my Week 2, and if what happened to me here in Billings earlier this morning is a portent of what's to come, maybe things will work out for me after all.

I was eating breakfast when a notification popped up on my phone. A stranger, recognizing my photo from the author pic on the back of *Dialogues with the Divine: Encounters with My Wisest Self* and thrilled at the possibility of chatting with the author of one of his favorite books, wanted to say hi. It's always gratifying to hear from readers, so I was happy to chat. When he learned that I was in his town on a road trip and was carrying copies for sale of all my books, he asked to meet so he could buy signed copies of my three *Q'ntana* fantasy novels. Twenty minutes later he was standing at my car in the hotel parking lot. Ten minutes after that, I had pocketed forty-eight dollars in cash.

On this journey, every dollar counts...as does every miracle.

BIG HORN CANYON NATIONAL RECREATION AREA, WYOMING
AFTERNOON

The day's second miracle sure didn't start out looking like one.

I've gotten into the habit of carrying deli cold cuts, grapes, apples, cherry tomatoes, baby carrots, an English cucumber, a hunk of cheese and a pack of crackers in my cooler and spreading them out in smorgasbord-like picnics at lunch and dinner — alfresco for lunch and in my hotel or motel room for dinner. It's cheaper than eating out, and it's always dog-friendly.

Most days, as midday approaches, I scout out nearby parks, picnic areas or other suitably lunchable spots; shade is particularly important at this time of year. That's what I was doing today on Main Street in Cowley, Wyoming (pop. 623), too preoccupied to notice the town's speed-limit sign.

When I'm driving, one of Kyri's favorite spots in my Prius is seated at attention on the console next to me, watching the world go by. That's where he was when, seemingly out of nowhere, a siren screamed by as a state trooper passed me and motioned me to stop.

I don't do well with authority figures in uniform. I do less well when my financial resources are alarmingly scarce.

The trooper went through the usual drill, taking my license and registration back to his car to check me out. When he returned, ticket book in hand, my heart sank. Before he could pull out his pen, he looked past me to Kyri, who grinned at him in that irresistible way all dogs have. Did the hardened trooper's heart melt at the sight? I don't know. Whatever happened in that instant, though, the ticket book disappeared, replaced by a chart of speeding fines. A frowning, super-stern warning later, Kyri and I were on our way… the hell out of Cowley…but slowly.

Day 9

Wednesday, June 5
WY-31 between Manderson & Hyatville, Wyoming

MID-MORNING

My plan for today (if I can ever be said to have one) was to head up into the Bighorn Mountains; first, to return to Medicine Wheel National Historic Landmark, then to look for the "mystery power spot" I mentioned here on Saturday.

The largest ancient Native American medicine wheel still intact — it could be more than three thousand years old — sits at 9,640 feet in these mountains, only twelve miles from where I'm sitting. The problem is that I'm sitting in my car and my car isn't moving. That's because a giant herd of cattle has spilled onto the road in front of me, with no more apparent interest in moving on than the motorcycle-riding cowboy up ahead seems to have in moving it on.

After fifteen minutes of inactivity, I decide that if the cattle won't move on, I will...though not to Medicine Wheel. At least not today. If I'm back in the area tomorrow, maybe I'll try again...or maybe not.

The good news is that my mystery power spot is no longer a mystery. How could I have forgotten that I wrote about it in *Acts of Surrender*? It's called Powder River Pass, and it's a couple of hours from here on US-16. That's where I'm headed.

Gillette, WY
EVENING

I was exploring the Bighorn Mountains in 1997, when I happened on a craggy rock formation on US-16 at Powder River Pass. There was nothing distinctive or scenic about it, and I had no plans to stop. But on that journey as on this one, I always endeavored to follow the voice of my intuition, and that voice urged me to pull into the small parking area in front of the barren, hundred-foot-high tor.

I opened the car door and Roxy scampered out and up the rocks; I followed behind, in something of a daze. It felt as though I was being whisked back in time…to the beginning of time itself, to a time of dragons, to a time before time. I stood motionless, the summer wind eddying around me, and I knew I had been here before, at the very timeless time I was sensing — as silly as it sounded to my logical mind. Moreover, I knew the dragons whose presence I felt, something else my logical mind was eager to dismiss. In that instant I knew, too, with every fiber of my beingness, that I was experiencing a form of genesis — the world's and mine.

If my second visit, nine years later, wasn't as dramatic, its magnetic, transformative power still washed over me. So when I realized I would be traveling east out of Portland, I knew I had to return.

The album *Ascension Harmonics* was streaming through my car stereo when I left my Greybull motel this morning for the Bighorn Mountains and, hopefully, Medicine Wheel and Powder River Pass. I hadn't been in Sedona long, back in 1997, when I stumbled on the *Ascension Harmonics* CD in a local bookstore. After I had listened to only a few minutes of the opening track, I knew I had to have it. In the twenty-two years since, I have probably listened to this Richard Shulman/Samuel Welsh recording more than nearly any other in my collection. I have meditated to it, fallen asleep to it, written to it, used it as background music for guided visualizations in my classes and workshops and, on this day, considered it to be the perfect soundtrack for my trek up into the mountains.

It was 11:22 when I pulled into the Powder River Pass parking lot, as the final bars of the album's final track faded into silence. Numbers carry their own frequency and energy, as music, itself a form of math, does. Repeating numbers amplify that effect. For

Ascension Harmonics to end at 11:22, just as I pulled into this incredibly powerful place, felt stunningly significant.

When I stepped out of the car, I began recording my thoughts and experiences on my phone. I transcribed it when I got to my hotel this afternoon...

I climb to the lower rocks with Kyri, sit down and shut my eyes. Immediately, I feel a sense of rapid movement...as though I'm flying... as though I'm an eagle in flight. Recalling my first time here and the dragon-energy I sensed back then, I listen for the voice of these ancient rocks, knowing they have a message for me, knowing they called me here to deliver that message.

"This journey is a pivot point for you...both an ending and a beginning. Returning to these rocks is a pivot point within this journey. Endings and beginnings. Beginnings and endings.

"This is a homecoming, yet it is also a launching pad, for your journey has barely begun...both this journey in your car and the journey that carries your words and work into the world. Surrender to it. Surrender to them. And continue this odyssey deep into the heart of all that you are and all that is.

"You fear what lies ahead. Do not. You worry that you will not be supported, that you will not be taken care of. Worry not. All is in place to ensure that all you have come to be and do will be carried out. Not always easily, but always miraculously.

"Remember the miracles. Open your heart and mind to the miracles. Embrace the miracles. And all will be well, as all already is.

"You have come to this place, again for the first time, to be reminded of all that you hold holy and of all the holiness and wholeness within you. As you leave — and leave you must, for there remain many more miles for you to travel — carry this place, this hallowed place, within you, as you have before and will again.

"Sit in the silence now. Inhale the sacredness of this place and of this time. When you have breathed it in, move on...into the rest of this day, into the rest of this life.

"Namaste."

Day 10

Thursday, June 6
RAPID CITY, SOUTH DAKOTA

LATE AFTERNOON

So much about this journey reminds me of the one I took from Toronto in 1997. I am even covering some of the same territory, if in reverse as I noted the other day.

Will I end up back in Toronto at the end of this? Improbable, but who knows? Although I don't see myself returning to Canada any time soon, there is little about my life that I could have predicted when I drove out of Toronto twenty-two years and thirteen days ago. Living in the US full-time? It would have seemed unlikely on that morning, yet twenty days later, I crossed the border and never went back. Becoming a US citizen? Even more unlikely, yet I swore the oath of allegiance eighteen months and three days ago, and I now have two passports: American as well as Canadian.

This afternoon, I took Kyri for a short hike in the Black Hills National Forest, a few miles outside Rapid City city limits. Unlike Roxy, his long-ago predecessor, Kyri is part-terrier and all-hunter. Roxy was no more obedient than Kyri, but as a cocker spaniel, food and trash were more appealing to her than living prey. Food and trash are largely stationary, which made Roxy easier to manage. Kyri, however, will chase after nearly anything, whether it has four legs or two wheels. So choosing to let him off leash on the trail felt like a giant risk. But that same intuition that has been guiding me thus far, effectively if not entirely stresslessly, encouraged me to untether him. He did great, never straying off the path, always remaining in full view and, most importantly, always coming when called.

I doubt I will ever let him off-leash again outside the confines of a dog park or other fenced-in area. Today, though, he was my surrogate — free, untethered and open to whatever the road has to reveal.

Day 11

Friday, June 7
CHAMBERLAIN REST STOP, SOUTH DAKOTA — EASTBOUND I-90

MID-AFTERNOON

I have pulled off eastbound I-90 at this rest stop for the usual reasons, for me and Kyri, but also because this is my first opportunity to get a good look at the Missouri River.

When you live in the desert, as I have for much of my time in the US, you forget the majesty and power of the great North American rivers. I grew up on one: the St. Lawrence, which links the North Atlantic with the Great Lakes and surrounds my hometown on the Island of Montreal. The Missouri, which I crossed about ten minutes ago, is the first major river I have seen since leaving the Columbia behind eight days ago in Central Washington.

The Missouri is more than a major river; it's the longest river in North America, flowing south for 2,341 miles before entering the Mississippi north of St. Louis. St. Louis, of course, is where I'm headed — not for the city but for another return visit, this time to the Gateway Arch. Crossing the Missouri feels like a foreshadowing of that.

Will I also cross the Mississippi when I get there and continue east? Or will I turn back west, toward I don't know where and I don't know what? It's pointless to ask these questions, but I can't help myself. Many of my books talk about the difference between "need to know" and "want to know," none more eloquently than *The Way of The Fool*, whose Step #10, "Embrace the Mystery," ends with this affirmation: "I, [insert your name], give up my need to know, surrender to the mystery and allow myself to be guided in faith as the Fool that I am. And so it is."

It's hard to give up the desire to know. It's hard to surrender to the mystery. It's hard to let myself be guided in faith as the Fool that I most definitely am. I guess that's why Step #10 thrust itself into *The Way of The Fool* and why it keeps showing up for me on this odyssey.

Not embracing the mystery demonstrates a lack of trust, and if this Fool's Journey is about anything for me, it's about trust. Deepening trust. More trust some days than I think I can marshal. Yet somehow I do because, in the end, what other choice do I have?

I, Mark David Gerson, give up my need to know, surrender to the mystery and allow myself to be guided in faith as the Fool that I am. And so it is.

Day 12

Saturday, June 8
CARTER LAKE, IOWA

EVENING

I passed a giant (and I mean giant) "Trump-Pence-'Make America Great Again'" banner today, plastered on an industrial building in Modale, Iowa. It was disturbing, but I didn't stop to take a picture of it because, well, I couldn't bring myself to.

Soon after, I was forced to take a detour to bypass Main Street because Modale was having a "family day" parade. It saddened me to think of all the families in that town who could not feel included in the celebration because they *would not* have been included in the celebration.

It's easy to forget, in the liberal cocoon that is Portland and the Pacific Northwest, where inclusion feels like a fact of life (although I'm certain that, to some, it doesn't feel that way at all), how excluded so many in this country can feel and how much they may feel they must hide for reasons of basic safety (including physical safety) and both job and housing security.

And it's hard not to wonder, as I travel through what sometimes feels like the heartless Heartland, how differently some people might respond (or react) to me if they knew I was gay and Jewish... not to mention an immigrant.

I'm lucky. My minorities are invisible. And, to date at least, I have always managed to live in places where I don't have to hide who I am to feel safe.

As I drove through Modale this afternoon, though, I thought

about all those who aren't so fortunate, a number that is increasing in this country and in too many others, given a climate that gives haters, including the violent among them, permission to act out their hate with impunity.

It's a reminder to those of us who can be open about who we are to *be* open, in every way we can. We owe it to those who can't.

Day 14

Monday, June 10
BLUE SPRINGS, MISSOURI

EARLY MORNING

I'm about thirty minutes west of Kansas City this morning, and I expect to be on the road to St. Louis within the next hour or two, as soon as I've finished breakfast and packed up Kyri and the car. Since leaving Portland two weeks ago, St. Louis is the only place, along with Wyoming's Bighorn Mountains, that I have felt strongly called to visit. Not for the city or anyone in it, but for its Gateway Arch.

The last time I was at Gateway Arch was two years ago on my sixty-third birthday. I had already been feeling the itch to leave Albuquerque after most of ten years, and I sought to anchor that by spending my birthday elsewhere. I wasn't looking to move to St. Louis, but for the purposes of the trip, I wanted to go somewhere as unlike the desert-y Southwest as possible. Only by removing myself from the energy and geography of the region where I had spent the bulk of my time in this country could I open to whatever and wherever might be next. St. Louis was the nearest place within driving distance that met those criteria and felt right.

I wasn't thinking about the Gateway Arch or its potential significance when I made the decision. Not consciously. But once I started planning, I realized that the Gateway Arch was a major reason — perhaps the prime reason — for my choice. I also realized that that's where I needed to spend at least part of my birthday.

Although I had no major epiphanies that day as I wandered the grounds with my camera and rode the tram to the Arch's 630-foot summit, I did on the drive back to Albuquerque. And soon after I returned, Portland emerged as my next best home. Remember "portal land"? Well, isn't the Arch a sort of portal? After all, it was built as a "gateway" between east and west, as a symbol of "westward expansion."

Now, apparently, I need another go at the Arch to complete the cycle I launched two years ago and to begin a new one. Maybe that's the key to whatever this journey is about and to wherever it will ultimately drop me.

My first experience of St. Louis was in December 2005, about a third of the way into that second Fool's Journey of mine. At the time, I wasn't doing much writing or photography. I was drawing my abstract/energetic impressions of the places I passed through. I created more than a hundred drawings over that thirty-three month span, mostly of natural phenomena. Occasionally, including in St. Louis, I felt the urge to draw something manmade. At the time, I described my Gateway Arch drawing as "an initiation into greater revelation and light," representing a gateway and portal to expanded consciousness.

I wonder what kind of initiation, gateway and/or portal I will encounter this time...

St. Louis, Missouri
LATE AFTERNOON

Kyri and I spent an hour or so wandering the grounds at the Gateway Arch this afternoon. Unlike in 2017, when the area immediately under the Arch was cordoned off for the construction of a new visitors center, this time I was able to walk through it. An arch is a portal, after all.

Now, I'm on a bench in Compton Hill Reservoir Park, a favorite St. Louis oasis about four miles away. My time at the Arch felt profound if subtle...too subtle for words, always frustrating for a writer. I need to sit with it for a bit. Maybe for longer than a bit. I hope to find the words to write about what happened; I don't have them yet.

Day 15

Tuesday, June 11
Mark Twain State Park, Missouri

NOON

It looks like I am not continuing east. For now, at least, the Mississippi River is as far east as I'm meant to go. At the same time, I wasn't ready to leave the Mississippi behind when I drove out of St. Louis.

After spending the night in O'Fallon, west of the city, I headed north as far as I could on MO-79, which parallels the river. Then I cut across to US-61, following it to Hannibal, Mark Twain's boyhood home and the setting for *Tom Sawyer* and *Huckleberry Finn*. From Hannibal, I took back roads to Mark Twain State Park and the Mark Twain Birthplace State Historic Site. I can't go inside the house he was born in; it's too hot to leave Kyri in the car. But I have found a bench a short walk away. It's shaded and overlooks Mark Twain Lake (everything around here is named after him).

As I gaze out over the lightly rippling water, I'm hoping that if some of the great writer's creative energy still permeates the place, I will absorb it by sitting here. His success energy, too.

I'm now about sixty miles west of the Mississippi, and when I get back behind the wheel in about twenty minutes, I expect to be putting more distance between me and the river. It's time to start making my way west again.

Day 17

Thursday, June 13
North Platte, Nebraska

EVENING

Three days have passed since the end of my second week on the road. In one sense, it's hard to believe I've been gone seventeen days. In another, my Portland life is galaxies away. The last visible reminder of that life is Kyri, who I rescued about halfway through my time there, days before my sixty-fourth birthday. Who's the rescuer now? If it weren't for Kyri's company, his cuddles, his unconditional love and all the ways he makes me smile, I doubt I would have made it this far.

Two weeks and three days... When I was planning my exodus, two weeks was all the time I figured I had before my cash and credit ran out. But here it is, Day 17, and I'm still standing...and driving.

I haven't shared this here before, at least not directly, although I've hinted at it, but the reason I left Portland so dramatically was financial. Simply put, I was pushed out for lack of funds. I was two weeks late with my rent, and I was facing certain eviction.

If I couldn't find a way to stay where I was, a semi-furnished rental in the Pearl District, I also lacked the wherewithal to make other arrangements. Nor had I been in Portland long enough to have developed the kind of friendships that could get me a free room or a couch while I tried to sort my life out. Even a homeless shelter, something I briefly considered, would have been challenging with Kyri.

If money, or a lack of it, was the surface reason for my departure, there were also deeper ones. There inevitably are, even if I can't always identify them. I hadn't been long out of the city when it became absolutely clear to me that I was on the right path, that if circumstances had pushed me out the other side of Portland's "portal land" portal, it was because it was time for me to move on… to take another Fool's leap into the unknown.

This journey is a leap of faith in so many ways. As I have noted here before, I rarely know from one day to the next where I'm going or where I'll end up. Not surprisingly, that's how I write: moment-by-moment and word-by-word, with little idea of the story, except as it unfolds. I never plan, plot or outline, and I always end up where I need to be. For nearly half my life, I have been pushed to live that way, too, although never as radically as this.

These days, the scariest leap comes in trusting that the resources I need to keep me going and, ultimately, to "land" me, will continue to manifest. That trust was seriously tested this afternoon, when I discovered that the pet deposit on my Portland condo would not be returned. That's no reflection on Kyri, who was and remains a model pup. It has to do with me breaking my lease. And there's nothing I can do about it.

My immediate response was panic. I had been counting on that five hundred dollars, and watching it evaporate over the course of a phone conversation was unnerving.

One of my core fears, and one that must go all the way back to childhood, is a fear of abandonment (how perfect that I adopted a rescue dog who mirrors that fear back at me daily). Yet if you have read *Acts of Surrender*, you know that I have never been abandoned. Magic and miracles have always shown up for me, and I have *always* been taken care of (although, as I've said, not necessarily in ways I would consciously choose). It took me a few hours of driving across the Nebraska emptiness today to remember that.

It *will* work out. It always has.

I *will* be fine. I always have been.

From the "A Little Validation Never Hurts" Dept: In certain traditions, the ladybug is viewed as a symbol of prosperity and good fortune. Not long after my conversation with the leasing agent, a ladybug landed in front of me at my rest stop picnic table Somehow, I will be fine.

From the "Every Cloud Has a Silver Lining" Dept: The same leasing agent who refused to refund my pet deposit promised to give me a stellar rental reference should I need one when I finally land. In the long run, that could prove more beneficial than the five hundred dollars, as handy as that would be right about now. Somehow, I will be fine.

Day 18

Friday, June 14
ROCK SPRINGS, WYOMING

MORNING

I don't have much to say about my time at the Gateway Arch in St. Louis. Despite feeling some ineffable "something" as I crossed under the Arch — first from east to west to symbolize my personal "westward expansion," then from west to east for new beginnings — I was disappointed not to have an immediate *aha*. This journey has been filled with such uncertainty that I was yearning for some dramatic and illuminating revelation. Another intuitive "lightbulb moment." The only certainty I felt was that I had traveled as far east as I needed to. I spent that night in the western suburbs of the city, and I have been on a westward-ish course ever since.

Now, I'm heading vaguely toward Reno, Nevada, which popped into my head as a destination (temporary? permanent?) on the drive out of St. Louis. But before I tell you about the drive out of St. Louis, let me backtrack to the drive *to* St. Louis.

Being keenly aware that my impending experience at the Gateway Arch would be pivotal in some way, I pondered where I might like to land once these travels come to an end. (Hopefully, they *will* come to an end.)

I didn't expect a Moses-like tablet to drop from the sky pinpointing precise GPS coordinates, although that would have been convenient. I was simply trying to intuit a vague geographic sense. What was I looking for? Did I want to live in a big city again? In a small town again? In the country again? Did I want to return to something like the embracing leafiness of the Pacific Northwest or to the rugged starkness of the high desert? Or did I want something new and different, perhaps a living situation, topography and/or part of the country that I had never experienced? Or would it be time to return to Canada?

I got an answer, but like so many I have received over the years, it wasn't what I was expecting.

A brief sidebar...

Frequently over the past year and a half, especially as my life in Portland began to constrict, I would go within to try to connect with my soul's yearning. What was it that was most important to me? What gave me the most joy? What made my heart sing? Which activity or activities best and most fully expressed my deepest passions? As these are the same kinds of questions I often ask my coaching clients, it was only fair to ask them of myself.

What emerged each time, with increasing clarity, was confirmation of an unshakable desire to tell my stories as the writer and storyteller I am and to be supported doing it, directly (book sales, screenplay proceeds, etc.) and through whatever related activities flow from it (i.e., coaching, teaching, speaking, etc.).

So, when I asked my location questions on the drive to St. Louis, I probably shouldn't have been surprised to hear this:

Stop searching for the place you want to live or think you want to live. That's not what this is about. Open your heart to the place that will support you in your heart's desire. Open your mind to the place that will free you to write and promote your books, that will support you in all the ways that matter — financially, creatively, emotionally and spiritually. Open to whatever that place is, however unlikely, unconventional or illogical it might seem.

To be clear, I am not clairaudient. Unlike some intuitives, I don't often hear "voices" speaking to me. Rather, my "hearing" has always been a deep inner knowingness — whether it's related to the stories I'm writing or, as in this case, the stories I'm living. Unfortunately, that knowingness rarely comes with any cues or evidence that might help me trust what I'm sensing.

What I "heard" that morning on eastbound I-70 felt monumental...and right. After all, if what most fully and deeply expresses my soul's yearning is to write and share my stories, then I would have to jettison my surface preferences and prejudices and surrender to the place that would be most likely to give me what I desire and require. So as I drove northwest into Iowa after my time at Gateway Arch and Mark Twain State Park, that's what I attempted to discern.

Assuming that North America was the geographic palette I was working with and using a blend of intuitive "tuning in" and kinesthetic muscle-testing, I first ran through each US and Canadian region, then narrowed it down to states (sorry, Canada) and metro areas. The unlikely result (after much checking, double-checking and triple-checking)? Reno.

Even as I always strive to act on my intuition, I still sometimes question it. I sure did with Reno.

Doubter that I was, I asked for a sign. "A license plate," I said to whatever disembodied energy or higher/wiser aspect of myself might be listening. "You've done it with license plates before. Do it again." (There's a story I tell in *Acts of Surrender* about Texas and license plates.)

So, all through the day's drive into Iowa, I watched for a Nevada license plate. Nothing. Same thing the following day as I drove across Nebraska.

Then something odd happened as I was pulling out of my motel parking spot yesterday morning: A white Porsche 911 blocked my way, and I had to stop to let it pass. For years, my dream car has been the Porsche 911, which has always symbolized success to me. With this 911 sighting, though, my first of the journey, I couldn't help but wonder whether the dream and the symbolism had lost their relevance. After all, here I was in North Platte, Nebraska, hardly a poster boy for anything resembling what the world views as success. I shrugged and left the parking lot, only to find myself following the Porsche for half a block until it turned off, seemingly into a Macdonald's.

When I rounded the corner and saw a gas station next to the McDonald's with attractively low fuel prices, I pulled in to one of the pumps. That's when I noticed the same Porsche at a neighboring pump. As I drove past it, I also noticed its license plate: Nevada. Perhaps more telling was the license plate frame, from *Zen* Auto.

Is it a sign? Does it mean I'm moving to Reno? I have no idea. All I can say is that once I got over my initial resistance and surrendered to the possibility of Reno as a landing place, the magic I talk about in *The Way of the Fool* amped up. Donations increased (one matched, dollar-for-dollar, my lost pet deposit), books sold and, more importantly, I was suddenly more optimistic than I had been in days about the outcome of this journey.

Maybe it isn't about Reno the city at all. Along with Powder River Pass, another of my "power places" is Pyramid Lake, about forty miles north of Reno on the Pyramid Lake Paiute Reservation. It's all that remains of the giant Pleistocene-era inland sea that once covered most of Nevada. Maybe I'm misreading the message and it's to Pyramid Lake I am being pulled, not to live but for a return visit.

That's the problem with "tuning in" in meditation, with "listening for the story" when we write or with any kind of channeling: The incoming message consists of energy, not words, and it's up to our brain to convert that energy into language, which it can only do based on our knowledge and experience. Moreover, when we are converting something infinite (energy) into something finite (words), the translation is always approximate. All of which to say, my "energy conversion" around Reno could be slightly off.

Regardless, I am choosing to head in that direction, and whatever Reno's call, I will definitely make my way to Pyramid Lake and endeavor to stay open to whatever shows up for me there...and along the way.

Day 21

Monday, June 17
Fernley, Nevada

MORNING

After the giant "Trump-Pence" banner that so disturbed me in Modale, Iowa earlier this month, it was heartening to drive through Heber City, Utah on Saturday afternoon and see the city decked out for Pride: Rainbow "Pride in the Wasatch Back" banners hung from every lamppost along Main Street.

When I mentioned that I was heading to Reno, one of my Facebook friends suggested I stay in nearby Fernley. Just off I-80, it's an easy drive either west to Reno or north to Pyramid Lake, making it a perfect home base for me in the area.

If there is something in Reno for me, it will have to wait until later today, though. My first outing after breakfast will be up to Pyramid Lake.

Pyramid Lake, Nevada
EARLY AFTERNOON

This is not the kind of lake you often see in Western states, the result of a dammed-up river. This lake is natural, fed at its southern end by the Truckee River. This is also not the kind of lake you see in the East or Midwest. There are no grassy verges, no groves of trees, no clusters of cottages, no stately resorts, no bobbing wooden docks, no noisy speedboats. No rowboats or canoes. No people.

Although camping, boating and fishing are permitted here, there's no sign of any activity.

Apart from the odd passing car, the peace here is absolute.

Apart from the steel blue of the still water, the deep blue of the cloud-streaked sky and the dun and sage shadings of the rocks and scrub, its world is colorless.

Yet the stark emptiness is neither ugly nor alienating. It has a numinous quality that makes it easy to understand why so many Native American sacred sites are scattered through the area.

In one of my past lives in this lifetime, I was a sound healer, using the vibrational power of my voice to shift energy and offer physical, emotional and spiritual relief. This healing modality, which went through numerous name changes over the years, evolved from the Reiki attunements I'd learned to do when I was initiated as a Reiki master on my first visit to Missoula. Traveling the country offering group and individual sessions was partly how I supported myself during my 2004-to-2007 journey, until my Muse stepped in and insisted I refocus my energy on writing. It enforced that "directive" by immediately cutting off all public demand for what had once been a thriving endeavor. Since then, apart from the occasional client, I have done all my sound work either on myself or when I have found myself in a particularly powerful place.

I had barely pulled into the first graveled parking area facing the lake, about five miles north of Nixon, when I sensed this to be such a place. I stepped out the car, turned to face the lake and, grateful that no one was around to hear, began to chant my peculiar vocalizations, which range in tone from grating to melodic. Was I singing to the lake or giving myself a healing? Both, probably. All I know is that when I felt complete, I returned to the car, backtracked past Nixon, and turned up the other side of the lake toward NV-445, the back road to Reno.

About a hundred yards past the Reno turnoff are a couple of covered picnic tables high on a rise overlooking the lake. Instead of continuing on to Reno, I stopped there for lunch, which is where

I'm writing this. Here, too, apart from the rare vehicle, the stillness is complete.

I'm not entirely sure what I experienced over on the other side of the lake. Whatever it was, it was transformational...as transformational as my stops at Powder River Pass and the Gateway Arch. I don't have to know how it was transformational. As always, I simply have to trust.

Reno, NV
MID-AFTERNOON

However strong the call felt a few days ago to come to Reno, it's muted now that I'm here. As I walk Kyri along the Truckee River path that winds through town, I don't feel much of anything, other than gratitude for whatever force brought me back to Pyramid Lake. I'm in the area for a couple of days, however, so Reno will have a few more opportunities to woo me.

Fernley, NV
EVENING

There are many reasons why I launched this Fool's Journey three weeks ago. The surface one, as I mentioned here previously, was the financial challenge that forced me out of my Portland rental and that made finding alternative accommodation problematic. As I have also mentioned, I have come to believe that this journey needed to happen regardless and that my money issue was the catalyst that forced my hand.

Why did it need to happen, and why have I already traveled thousands of miles on this odyssey? Here's what I know, although what I don't yet know (and may never entirely know) is, as always, far vaster...

- This is my fourth open-ended Fool's Journey road trip, and each of its predecessors presaged a radical life change I could never have predicted. No doubt, this one will do something similar. (I write about the others in *Acts of Surrender*.)

- If my spiritual journey consists of one leap of faith after another, each more daring than the last, this is my most daring to date, forcing me to surrender to my intuition and to trust my inner knowingness in ways I never believed possible.
- I'm a storyteller, and this journey is turning into one hell of a story. As I tell it, I'm letting myself be more publicly vulnerable than I have in the past. It's scary but satisfying, not least because...
- I write my stories to inspire as well as entertain, and it's clear from the comments on my posts that my journeying is inspiring others in many of the same the ways it inspires me. And as I share it with the people I meet along the way, it inspires them as well.

None of this is altogether new. In one way or another, these are all ongoing themes in my life.

What was new occurred a few days into this journey as I was sharing the story behind my first novel with a friend.

Although I began writing *The MoonQuest* in Toronto, I suspended work on it after a few months when I felt powerfully impelled to sell everything I then owned, buy my first car (at age thirty-nine) and move a thousand miles east to Nova Scotia, a place where I knew no one. (That was 1994 and a different kind of Fool's Journey.)

It would be six months before I felt able to pick up the manuscript again. What I would come to realize was that I had needed those six months of radical life change to grow into *The MoonQuest*'s story enough to be able to finish it. Twenty-five years later, is this Fool's Journey serving a similar creative purpose?

Earlier this year, I started then almost immediately suspended work on an unexpected fourth story in my *Q'ntana* fantasy series (*The MoonQuest* was the series' first). It's as though the moment I surrendered to this unexpected new installment in the series was the moment this current journey became inevitable.

Of course, I can't know what it is about these travels that will feed this as-yet-untitled fourth *Q'ntana* story. I may never know specifically, any more than I know what about my move to Nova Scotia fed *The MoonQuest*.

Yet I feel it in my heart to be true, and I can't wait until it's time to get back to it so I can find out what this new story is about. Maybe then I will also find out what this Fool's Journey story is about.

Day 22

Tuesday, June 18
Reno, Nevada

AFTERNOON

I'm sitting at Dolan Toyota waiting for my Prius (aka the Foolmobile) to get its twenty-thousand-mile servicing. Maybe that's all Reno was ever about...because not much else has happened here (at least not that I've noticed), apart from my outing to Pyramid Lake. Reno has a few hours left to make an impression; I hit the road again in the morning.

Speaking of the road, guess how many miles I've driven over the past three weeks. There's no way I would have guessed right, and I only know because I snapped a picture of my odometer once Portland was behind me. Then, it read 13,614, which means I've traveled some seven thousand miles in barely three weeks. Put another way, I have averaged a cosmic-sounding 333 miles a day.

Fernley, Nevada
EVENING

When I leave here in the morning to continue this open-ended odyssey, I'll be marking the twenty-second anniversary of the start of my first.

On June 19, 1997, I left Toronto with my dog, with everything I owned packed into my Dodge Caravan and with no fixed destination. Three months later, after having covered some of the same territory I'm covering now, if in reverse order, I landed in

Sedona, Arizona. I had no plans to stay more than a couple of days and expected Sedona to be another whistle-stop on the road to wherever. Instead, one week grew to two, one month to seven. Before I knew it, I had a new country and a new wife, and a new baby was on the way. It was a life I could never have imagined, and on the eve of this anniversary it reminds me that it's pointless to try to figure out where I'm headed or why. All can do, yet again, is trust in the journey.

We'll see where it carries me tomorrow.

Day 23

Wednesday, June 19
KLAMATH FALLS, OREGON

EARLY EVENING

When I noted last night that I had no idea where I'd be heading today, I couldn't have imagined I would find myself back in Oregon some twenty-four hours later. Yet here I am.

That's the thing about this journey, and about my writing as well as my life: There is little about the way any of these has played out that I could have imagined, predicted or even consciously thought I wanted. Not in my wildest fantasies. So, to recap what I wrote last night, there's no point trying to figure out where this journey is taking me, let alone where it's taking me tomorrow. As it has done over these past twenty-three days, it will take me where I need to go, if I let it.

LATE EVENING

T'was grace that brought us safe thus far
And grace will lead us home.

I never paid much attention to the lyrics of "Amazing Grace" before today. Maybe I never needed to before today.

You see, when I got up this morning, I discovered that the credit card I had been using to cover my accommodations on this Fool's Journey was nearly maxed out, even though I paid the bill last week. Without paying it down some more, all I'd be able to manage was one more night's shelter, thanks to hotel reward points.

To my surprise, I didn't immediately freak out. I was definitely concerned, but I didn't plunge into panic…something I might have done not too many days ago.

What helped were a couple of fragments I remembered from a dream I had last night.

In the dream, I'm in a blinding snowstorm. All I can see around me is snow, and I have no idea which direction will take me to some sort of shelter. Somehow, though, and I don't now remember how, I get to safety. When I do, I hear this: "You were never in any real danger."

For all the dream reassured me early on, its effect faded pretty quickly once I was back on the road. Then out of nowhere, the word "grace" popped into my head and I remembered all the grace that has surrounded not only the twenty-three days of this journey but the nearly sixty-five years of my life.

It was then that I felt moved to play "Amazing Grace." This time, for the first time, I listened closely to the lyrics, and when I heard the lines I quoted above, my eyes filled with tears.

Grace *has* brought me "safe thus far." And I have to trust that grace will also lead me home — to my next physical home, of course, but more importantly, to the home in my heart.

I keep returning to *The Way of the Fool* here because it's a book, as I mention often, that I am being challenged to live more and more fully (Fool-ly) and more and more authentically each day.

Every one of the twelve and a half steps detailed in the book speaks to today's experience and to the totality of this open-ended road odyssey. However, these seven stand out as extra-relevant to me…

- STEP #3. Follow Your Heart
- STEP #7. Take Risks
- STEP #8. Live Your Passion
- STEP #9. Don't Give Up
- STEP #10. Embrace the Mystery

- STEP #11. Embrace the Magic
- STEP #12. Remember Who You Are

When I follow my heart, take risks, live my passion, refuse to give up, embrace the magic and mystery and remember who I am, grace cannot fail to come into play in my life...as it has and will continue to. I know that. The challenge is to remember it.

I *am* safe, and I am *never* in any real danger.

So be it. And so it is.

Day 24

Thursday, June 20
OR-62, near Fort Klamath, Oregon

NOON

In keeping with the "transformation" theme that has come up here more than once, including the other day at Pyramid Lake, a giant butterfly landed next to me a few minutes ago as I was enjoying a picnic lunch on my way to Crater Lake. It didn't stick around long enough for me to take its picture, but it felt like a positive sign that, despite my frequent anxiety, I'm on the right track. (Because of their metamorphosis from caterpillar, butterflies represent transformation in many traditions.)

Crater Lake National Park, OR
AFTERNOON

Until you have visited Crater Lake in south-central Oregon, you have not experienced the color blue. Not true blue. Crater Lake's blue is richer and more intense than any you are ever likely to see in another other body of water, or perhaps anywhere. That's because this lake, the deepest in the US, is one of the cleanest and clearest on earth. All its water comes from rain and snow. In other words, no inlets carry water into it from other sources, so it's free of all sediment and mineral deposits.

If my lunchtime butterfly symbolized for me the transformation I am experiencing on this journey, Crater Lake must symbolize depth and clarity, not to mention freedom from outside influence.

And communication. In eastern traditions, the chakras are the body's seven energy centers, each of which is associated with a note on the musical scale and a color. For the throat chakra, the note is G and the color, blue. The throat chakra represents voice, creative expression, authenticity and speaking one's truth.

And magic. Crater Lake's largest island, the remains of a volcanic cinder cone, is *Wizard* Island.

And creation. Long before I knew how Crater Lake was formed — when the twelve-thousand-foot Mount Mazama volcano erupted and collapsed — I liked to think of it as Cr(e)ator Lake. Although that eruption occurred nearly eight thousand years ago, today's Crater Lake continues to evoke the energy of new creation for me.

I wasn't thinking about any of that, at least not consciously, when I decided to drive up here this morning. I simply remembered it as being spectacularly beautiful and thought it would make a pleasant outing. It is and it did. Now, being here, it's so much more. It's hard to leave, but I have a three-hour drive ahead of me, to Eugene where I'll be meeting a longtime Facebook friend, in person for the first time.

Eugene, OR

EVENING

As I was driving to Starbucks this morning, I was reflecting on my time in Nevada and thinking that I was glad to be gone from there. No particular reason; that's just what popped into my head.

Yet when I spoke it out loud, this is what came out of my mouth: "I'm really glad I'm gone from Oregon." Of course, I'm still in Oregon or, more accurately, *back* in Oregon. But I have to wonder whether it was some sort of Freudian slip representing what I was deeply feeling, if not consciously acknowledging.

Tomorrow, I'm heading into Portland to check my post office box and drop by the Multnomah County Arts Center. Before I knew my life in Portland was coming to an end, I entered an excerpt from *Acts of Surrender* into the arts center's multimedia Pride exhibition.

To my amazement, my entry, the coming out chapter titled "Gay and Jewish" was juried in. Unfortunately, by the time the exhibit opened, I had already left town.

Although I'm excited to see my words up on the wall, I wonder how it will feel to be back in the city. Will I be nostalgic or homesick? Will I feel complete? Or will I have a sense of unfinished business? Part of me would prefer to avoid Portland along with those questions. I guess that's why I have to go.

Day 26

Saturday, June 22
CHEHALIS, WASHINGTON

LATE EVENING

A postscript to what I shared about "amazing grace" from Klamath Falls a few days ago…

It turns out that grace truly *is* amazing. To recap what I wrote on June 19, I had just learned that the credit card I have been using for my accommodations on this journey was nearly maxed out. At the time, I believed I had enough hotel reward points for one free night. I didn't know how I would manage beyond that.

Well, like the miracle of the Hanukkah story where oil sufficient for a single night miraculously lasted for eight nights, my reward points have also miraculously stretched themselves.

That evening, I discovered I had enough points for not one free night, but two. The next morning, in chatting with an agent at the rewards call center about a different issue, I learned about a new promotion, which immediately netted me enough additional points for two more free nights. And that evening, my first freebie, I had so many problems with the room that the manager refunded me the points I had used to pay for it. Within twenty-four hours, my points had multiplied enough to score me as many five free nights.

My miracle may not have been as dramatic as the one in the Hanukkah story; it was miracle enough for me.

I may not know how I'm going to sustain this journey into another month, but thanks to the miracle of amazing grace, it looks like I'm going to make it through this one. If I have learned anything on the greater Fool's Journey that is my life, it's that tomorrow has a way of taking care of itself. So I'll do my (imperfect) best not to worry.

Day 28

Monday, June 24
BOISE, IDAHO

MORNING

I didn't know what to expect when I drove into Portland on Friday, my first time back in the city since my May 28 exodus. Would I feel sadness? Regret? Relief? Would it be traumatic? Stressful? Depressing?

Initially, it was none of that.

My first stop that morning was Multnomah Village, where the arts center that's hosting the Pride exhibit featuring my *Acts of Surrender* excerpt is located. It's also a few minutes' drive from the first place I lived in Portland: a house-sit that transitioned into a room rental. I felt no emotional charge while in the area. Was I really at peace with the whole Portland experience?

Apparently not. A while later, when I exited the 405 and drove up the ramp into the Pearl District, my old center-city neighborhood, I burst into tears. And as I ran my errands in the area, I was overcome with emotion. I missed living there. I felt like a failure. It felt like home and not home, all at the same time. It felt familiar and alien, all the same time. I wanted to stay and I wanted to leave, all at the same time. It was no easier when I crossed the Columbia River out of Oregon at the end of the afternoon.

But as I walked Kyri the next morning in Chehalis, Washington, I had a revelation: Most of what I had been feeling in the Pearl had not been regret. It had been grief, though not for Portland and my life there. It had been grief for the parts of me I had left behind, old parts that could not continue into whatever new life I was moving into through this journey.

With that *aha*, I experienced a sense of completion that I hadn't on May 28: I had now fully passed through to the other side of Portland's "portal land" portal and surrendered into the new, however that might show up.

Later that morning, as I was driving east toward Yakima on US-12, a road that parallels my May 28 I-84 exit route, I reflected on what this "new life" might look like. What had I left behind? What was I stepping into? What was my heart's desire for this new chapter?

Whatever else might have changed post-Portland, one essential thing had not. I still felt a powerful core yearning to be free to write, tell and share my stories, stories that come from my heart and touch others. In that moment, a meditative vision I'd had fourteen years earlier flashed into my awareness.

Back then, it was a disturbing vision because it suggested the dissolution of a marriage that had yet to show any sign of ending. In the vision, I saw myself in my writing studio in a breathtaking home overlooking the Pacific. Problem was, I lived there alone; no wife, no daughter. That was the vision; the waking reality kicked in a month later when my wife revealed that she had fallen in love with someone else and that our marriage was over. Six months after that on the thirty-three-month journey that was precipitated by the marriage breakup, I stumbled onto a real-life version of the house of my vision, in Laguna Beach, California. I have loved Laguna Beach ever since.

This time when that vision floated back into my awareness, it flooded me with joy. The joy wasn't merely about writing. It was about writing in a place I have always loved and in a space that inspires me, in a place where I feel fully supported.

My intuition has guided me to live in many places over the years. Sometimes, I was excited to go. Sometimes, I was resistant. Sometimes, I was baffled. Sometimes, I was terrified. Sometimes, I got there before I realized I was to stay. Always, it proved to be the right place at the right time, even when it felt impossibly difficult.

Yet not in a single instance did I feel the same overpowering bliss I felt Saturday morning at the thought of being a fully supported writer in Laguna Beach.

The problem, of course, is that Portland stripped me bare and Laguna Beach is more expensive than Portland. How could I possibly transition from a day-to-day existence on the road to a full-time writing life in Laguna Beach? "Act as though and make it so," I write in *Acts of Surrender.* But by the time I got to Yakima that afternoon and noticed the state of my credit cards as I went to gas up my car, it didn't seem possible to "act as though." None of it seemed possible.

"Remember the feeling," I kept hearing through my mounting despair. "Remember the joy." Then, for the umpteenth time from *The Way of the Fool,* "Embrace the magic" (Step #11). Then, from *The Way of the Imperfect Fool,* "Take a chance" (Step #5) and "Do it now" (Step #6.)

In the hours since, that's what I have been endeavoring to do. In some moments, I succeed. In others, the conventional illogic of the proposition takes over and I can't.

At first, I was going to continue driving east for the time being because even when I was able to feel the joy, I couldn't see how I could afford to spend a single night in the Laguna Beach area, let alone settle there as a full-time (and Fool-time) writer. But when I left Othello, Washington yesterday morning (punster that I am, I like to call it the "hamlet of Othello"), the car pulled me southward, which is why I find myself in Boise as I write this, fully expecting my folly to continue to push me toward Southern California.

What will I do if that's where I end up? No clue. All I can do, as I have done throughout this Fool's Journey and in the years leading up to it, is muster enough trust to take whatever leaps of faith are demanded of me. That doesn't mean I'm not terrified. I often am. It does mean I can't let my terror paralyze me in all the ways it did in my teens and twenties.

What about Reno? Last week, I felt powerfully drawn there as the place that would support me and my writing. Yet once I got there, those feelings dissipated. Perhaps there was some energy there I needed to integrate or radiate, and once that was done so was Reno. Perhaps it was all about Pyramid Lake. Perhaps it was something else. Could the same happen in Laguna Beach? Could this feeling about Laguna vanish once I get there? Before I get there? Of course. Spirit/God/Muse is nothing if not a trickster. However, until I am guided otherwise, that's where I'm heading...though probably not directly to the house of my vision. Last time I checked, nine years ago, it had recently sold for twelve million dollars.

A few Laguna Beach postscripts...

- Last time I was in Southern California, in 2017 for my daughter's high school graduation, so much about Los Angeles felt funky that when I got home to Albuquerque, I was convinced that my longstanding dream of moving to LA had died. Apart from my time with my daughter, the only day that had felt powerfully positive was the one I spent in Laguna Beach with my friend Adam.

- As I was revisiting that fourteen-year-old vision on the drive to Yakima, I thought about the barely started fourth book in my *Sara Stories* series of novels. What would happen, I wondered, if Bernie (its main character) ended up in Laguna Beach? (One reason I hadn't been working on the book was that I didn't yet know where to place Bernie, who would be about my age in the final book of the series.) The instant that possibility entered my awareness, I started to cry.

- That afternoon, as I was sharing my realizations on the phone with Adam, he reminded me that it was in Newport Beach, a few miles up the coast from Laguna, that I had begun work on this fourth *Sara* book.

Later, I remembered that the same day I started working on the book, I'd wandered through Laguna Beach with Adam, collecting info on local galleries for the Bernie character, who is an artist in the series. Apparently, I'd already been thinking about placing Bernie there back then. None of this is proof of anything. The human spin we place on the signs, signals and synchronicities we encounter is not always the correct one, as I noted a while ago. Witness Reno. At the same time, on a journey like this, my human spin is often all I have to go on.

For now, I will try to stay connected to the joy I felt on Saturday. After all, if anything will fuel my dreams, it's the joy. And as long as I sense the joy to be moving me toward Laguna Beach, that's the direction I will travel.

ELKO, NEVADA
LATE AFTERNOON

Miracle du jour: This morning's writings about Laguna Beach sparked the most generous donation I have received to date. Plus, I sold three copies of *The Way of the Fool* to my hotel manager here when I checked in. Let the flow continue!

EVENING

I was so excited by my "miracle day" that I took myself out for ice cream after dinner. Unfortunately, I didn't choose to leave the ice cream parlor by the door. Instead, I smashed my face into a plate glass window. Definitely a big ouch. The good news is that apart from a nosebleed, a major (temporary) ache and some (very temporary) minor disorientation, I was fine.

Strangely, I did something similar fourteen years ago in Sedona, when I attempted to walked onto a hotel patio from its breakfast room without realizing that someone had shut the glass slider.

Is there a deeper meaning to these "collisions"? If so, it eludes me. Maybe I simply need to pay more attention to where I'm going.

LATE EVENING

Tomorrow marks the start of my fifth week on this Fool's Journey.

Are my travels drawing to an end as I surrender to the magnetic pull of Laguna Beach? Or will Laguna be nothing more than another way station on this journey? All I know is that I plan to continue heading west, until I feel otherwise guided...or until west ends at the Pacific.

Day 29

Tuesday, June 25
COSGRAVE REST AREA, NEVADA — WESTBOUND I-80

EARLY AFTERNOON

I forgot to mention this yesterday morning: In the ocean-view writing studio of my vision, I was working on a screenplay. Well, as I was driving west along I-80 a bit ago, I remembered that when I began (then immediately suspended) work on that fourth *Q'ntana* story, it was as a screenplay, not as a novel.

So, in case anyone is listening, I would be thrilled to return to work on the script in that stunning Laguna writing studio, or somewhere similar.

A guy can dream, can't he?

FERNLEY, NEVADA
LATE EVENING

In the wake of my recent Laguna Beach revelations and because I was going to be in the area anyhow, it felt appropriate to mark the start of my fifth week on the road with a return visit to Pyramid Lake.

It was nearly four in the afternoon when I checked back into my same Fernley hotel, late enough that I didn't bother to haul anything into my room from the car. Instead, I headed straight for Pyramid Lake and that same parking pull-off I stopped at eight days ago. (Was it only eight days? As I write this, it feels like lifetimes.)

My last experience at the lake was so powerful that I doubted this one could compete. Besides, the late afternoon sun was brutal and there was no shade. If I could handle the heat, for a while at least, Kyri probably couldn't. Our time there would have to be brief.

Yet as I stood gazing into the water and across at the pyramid-like Anaho Island (while Kyri tried to catch bees), this experience felt even more powerful than its predecessor. Once again, I didn't experience any obvious *aha*. But I sensed that whatever energies had called me back were working through my mind, body and spirit. I knew something within me had shifted.

Had it shifted enough for me to manifest my Laguna Beach dream? Or had it shifted me past that dream and into a new one? I couldn't know and still don't. For now, my plan hasn't changed. In the morning, I will get back onto I-80 and point the car toward California.

Day 30

Wednesday, June 26
FERNLEY, NEVADA

MORNING

It's Presidents' Day weekend 2005, I have been on the road for two months, and for the past week I have been staying at a Howard Johnson Express in Albuquerque. I have just paid for my stay to date and extended it by another couple of days. However, when I get back to my room and log into my bank account, I discover that the original authorization that went into effect when I checked in has not been lifted. In other words, with the original authorization, the payment I made and the new authorization, my account is overdrawn. *Seriously* overdrawn.

Although I know the red numbers on the screen will turn black on Wednesday morning once the authorization lifts and everything sorts itself out after the holiday weekend, it's hard not to freak out. On the surface, I appear to have no money.

I know that the appearance of lack is an illusion, yet illusions can be simultaneously compelling and disturbing, and I spend a somewhat anxious weekend.

Fast-forward to yesterday...

I log into one of my credit card accounts, expecting the payment I made on Friday to be reflected in my available balance. It isn't. In fact, I have barely enough available for gas, never mind tonight's accommodation.

Less freaked out than I expect to be (and less freaked out than I was fourteen years ago), I call Visa and my bank. The bank insists the payment was made; Visa insists they never received it. In all the many years I've been using my bank's bill pay, nothing like this has ever happened to me.

Visa promises to issue a temporary credit for the amount I paid while waiting for me to send proof of payment. Unfortunately, the temporary credit won't show up for two to three business days. My bank promises proof of payment, but it will take three to five business days to generate and get to me.

Now would be a good time to freak out.

To my surprise, I don't. A little juggling (made possible by some "amazing grace") will buy me the time I need until this gets fixed. I keep breathing and get on with my day.

What's the lesson in this for me?

The superficial lesson is to always take note of the confirmation numbers the bank spits out when I schedule a bill payment. Common sense, right? I used to do it, but after so many problem-free years, I lost the habit.

The deeper lesson, the same one I experienced at the Howard Johnson Express in Albuquerque, is that lack is an illusion. Somehow, often at the very, very, very last minute, I am always taken care of. Even though it has sometimes (too often) felt as though all is lost, as though I have been abandoned, it has never proven to be true. Never. Not once. In the moment (the only one that ultimately matters), I have always had all that I need.

Here's what I know (and try to remember, especially on this journey): If I continue on this Fool's path, if I continue to surrender to what I know in my heart to be true (despite outward appearances), if I continue to trust (more and more deeply with each passing day) and if I continue to take the leaps of faith my wisest self demands of me, I will always be okay. For when have I not been?

And the journey continues...

Day 31

Thursday, June 27
ANDERSON, CALIFORNIA

MORNING

I woke up this morning in a bit of a panic. Call it California sticker shock. That's because I spent part of yesterday evening exploring the cost of pet-friendly accommodation in Laguna Beach and Orange County. *Wow!* Then I looked up pet-friendly accommodation in and near Mount Shasta, one of the places I'm considering heading to today. Not as big a shocker, but still a shocker.

Only as I write this do I realize that my panic came about from breaking a cardinal rule of any Fool's Journey, which is to stay in the moment. It's right there in *The Way of the Fool*. Step #2: "Be In the Moment."

Here's what it says in the book...

"Focus on now — on this breath, on this moment, on this experience. Don't worry about tomorrow's or about any of the choices or decisions waiting for you next week or next month or next year.

"Trust all future breaths, moments and experiences to take care of themselves...and of you. And they will."

This journey continues to teach me. Pushing me into an even deeper practice of moment-to-moment living is certainly one of its greatest (and least comfortable) gifts.

As I've mentioned previously, this is my fourth open-ended Fool's Journey, and each has required of me more vision and faith than its predecessor. Much more. Each succeeding journey has also called on me to *know* (not merely believe) that in following my heart, I will always be taken care of, despite overwhelming logic to the contrary.

So, here I am in California, among the most expensive places in the country to travel, let alone live, and I'm feeling called to do both.

"If anyone can do it," a friend said to me this morning, "you can."

Deep down, I know he's right. But at 6:30 AM, that certainty can be difficult for me to access. Fortunately, once I drag myself out of bed, get dressed, walk Kyri and eat breakfast, I'm generally in better emotional shape. Writing also helps.

As for today, I feel pulled northwest (not to the Northwest). I'll have more certainty once I pack up dog and car and fuel up with coffee for the road.

And tonight? No idea. It's not this morning's concern. It will take care of itself, somehow, as it always has.

The same will have to be true for Laguna Beach, should the call to be there remain strong in the coming days.

All I know, all I have to know, is that in this moment I'm okay.

MID-MORNING

One of the most profound *aha*'s of this journey has been this: As I travel and find myself supported through donations and other forms of kindness, I see that the universe is supporting me not for what I do or for what I sell, but for who I am.

That doesn't diminish the value of the books I write and the coaching services I offer. At the same time, it places them where they belong, reminding me that my human "being" will always take precedence over my human "doing."

Day 32

Friday, June 28
ANDERSON, CALIFORNIA

EVENING

Mount Shasta is another of those power places that keeps drawing me back. I was there twice toward the end of my 1997 journey and again in 2006. The first time, fresh from my Reiki mastery in Missoula, I offered Reiki attunements to random people I ran into, performing those powerful activations both high on the mountain and down in town at the headwaters of the Upper Sacramento River.

At the time, offering Reiki attunements as healings was controversial as, traditionally, they are performed only during the initiation of new Reiki masters. But my Reiki mastery came with the certainty that I was to break tradition, and it was those attunements that quickly evolved into the beginnings of my sound-healing work. It was during my second Shasta visit, less than a week after the first, that I knew I had to make my way to Sedona, although I couldn't then imagine how life-changing that next stop would turn out to be.

Today's outing, like other of my power-place pilgrimages in recent weeks, did not lead to any instant revelations. It would have been helpful to have driven off with a clear sense of purpose and direction. Yet although I felt subtle inner shifts as I walked Kyri around the snowy patches at the Bunny Flat trailhead, the highest it was possible to drive today, no commandment-filled tablets were handed down to me up there, despite the 6,950-foot elevation.

About that snow... I tried to avoid stepping into it. Not Kyri. He dove into it with high-spirited abandon, gobbling up mouthfuls of the white stuff as he did. This wasn't Kyri's first snowy adventure; that was back in Portland. But every one is the same for him: a gleeful romp and doggy snow-cone snack. Among his many gifts to me is the reminder of how easy it can be to find joy in simple things.

I'm back in Anderson now, lounging in an Adirondack chair and listening to the tinkle-plash of a fountain as the golden glow of twilight slowly fades. Kyri is snoozing in the chair next to mine.

Of all the hotels and motels I have stayed in since leaving Portland, this is the most restful. It's on a quiet residential street and is perched on a low rise above the Sacramento River. If I could stay here for a week, I would. But the road is calling, and I will be back on it in the morning, headed for Hayward in the Bay Area.

Tomorrow night, for the first time on this odyssey, I won't be in a hotel or motel. A Facebook friend I've never met and with whom I've had minimal online contact has offered me and Kyri a bed for the night as his way of demonstrating support for my Fool's Journey. How can I doubt that I'm being taken care of?

Day 34

Sunday, June 30
PASO ROBLES, CALIFORNIA

MORNING

From shortly after I left Sedona in late 2004 until 2017 when I drove to LA for my daughter's high school graduation, there was always a tug-of-war within me between New Mexico and Southern California.

New Mexico won the first round in 2007, when after thirty-three months of Fool's journeying, I stopped in Albuquerque and stayed. Yet Southern California never fully left my consciousness or my heart as an ultimate destination.

Three years later in a series of synchronistic events that I chronicle in *Acts of Surrender*, I found myself propelled to LA in what, until then, was my biggest leap of faith. For ten weeks I stayed with a friend in Orange County, splitting much of my time between Laguna Beach and Los Angeles — exploring, working on drafts of *The StarQuest* and *Acts of Surrender* and waiting for the miracle that would make it possible for me to settle more permanently in the area.

The miracle never came. Instead, the pressure cooker that was my living situation grew more and more intense. A week after my fifty-sixth birthday, I left, with little sense of where I would end up or how I would finance the next chapter of my life. I was just about as broke the day I drove away as I had been when I arrived, and no better off than I was a month ago when I left Portland.

To my astonishment, a different series of miracles (not at all resembling the ones I had been expecting or hoping for) landed me back in Albuquerque, where for the next seven years I experienced a creative tsunami: I wrote nine new books, finished two others, published new editions of two other ones and revised and released two previously unpublished manuscripts. I also wrote four screenplays and penned early drafts of three stage musicals. Through that time, LA continued to tug at me...until that 2017 trip, where everything felt off, except for my day in Laguna and, of course, my time with my daughter.

A few months later, when I returned to Albuquerque from my birthday trip to St. Louis, I knew my time in New Mexico was drawing to an end. But with Los Angeles apparently out of the picture, where was I to go? That's when Portland happened.

Not for the first time in my life, I felt guided to move somewhere that I assumed was to be my long-term new home. Not for the first time, my assumption proved to be wrong.

I have now been gone from Portland for a month, still waiting for the call of my next place as I travel the roads of my soul's yearning. A week and half ago, it felt that it might be Reno. After my time at Pyramid Lake, Reno removed itself from the running. Then, I felt a pull to Laguna Beach. Now, thanks to Mount Shasta, I'm not sure about that either.

More accurately, perhaps, it was the drive up to Mount Shasta that precipitated the shift. As I left Anderson and wove north past Redding through heart-stoppingly stunning scenery, I wondered whether Laguna had shown up merely as a stepping stone to Los Angeles. "*I'm* where you need to be," LA seemed to be shouting at me. "I'm where you *want* to be."

It wasn't generic LA that was calling me back. It was Beverly Hills. Again.

Back in 2010, as my departure from Albuquerque drew nearer, I experienced more Beverly Hills-related synchronicities than I could list here. And once I began visiting Beverly Hills during my day trips up to LA from Orange County, it felt one hundred percent right to be there. More right than anywhere else in the area. More financially impossible, of course, but more right.

In one of her memoirs, *Wrinkle in Time* author Madeline L'Engle jokes about all the Old Testament prophets who looked up at the sky and shouted to God, "You want me to do what!?"

That's how I felt Friday on the road to Mount Shasta, when that intuitive sensing filtered up into my conscious awareness. On a journey where I am relying on the kindness of far-flung friends (most of whom I have never met) to keep me going, my limited mind couldn't imagine how I could make it as a full-time writer in Laguna Beach, let alone Beverly Hills. "Inconceivable!" it shouted, echoing Vizzini in *The Princess Bride*.

If you've seen the film, you know that every event Vizzini describes as inconceivable turns out to be possible. From that perspective, could Beverly Hills also be possible?

I don't have to know how. I don't have to know why. All I have to do is surrender to the possibility, continue to listen to the voice of my heart, continue to heed the counsel of my soul and continue to allow the requisite miracles to show up in whatever ways serve my highest good. That is the Way of the Fool.

Of course, Beverly Hills could prove to be a stepping stone of its own to something/somewhere else. Time will tell.

As for tonight, I'm in Paso Robles on California's Central Coast. Tomorrow, I will drive south to Irvine (as near to Laguna Beach as my accommodation funds will allow) and see what unfolds there for me. Beyond that? That's a question I won't need answered until Friday morning when it's time, once again, to move on.

July 2019

An artist has to trust his gut, his heart, his intuition.
After Sara's Year

Feel your fear. Then pass through it to the other side, where your destiny awaits.
The MoonQuest

Day 36

Tuesday, July 2
IRVINE, CALIFORNIA

MORNING

I woke up this morning to Week 6 of this journey and to my first Southern California morning in two years. It's not LA, it's not Laguna Beach, and Irvine isn't a coastal community. Yet it feels right to be here, even though I hit rush hour traffic as I made my way through LA yesterday, and the trip down the 405 into Orange County was more of a crawl than a drive.

What does it mean to be in Southern California? What will do now that I'm here? No idea. But I have until I check out on Friday morning to find out. So, once again, I need to find a way to stay in the moment.

LAGUNA BEACH, CA
NOON

I haven't wandered through Laguna Beach in two years, and it's good to be somewhere I can imagine as home, "home" having been an alien concept since before I left Portland. This is nice, even should it turn out to be temporary.

It's also wonderful to be this close to the Pacific. I caught glimpses on my way to Hayward the other day, but that was from the car or viewed in the distance from a vista point. Here, it's close enough to walk to, to dip my toes into, although I won't be able to do that today. Dogs aren't permitted on the beach this time of year, at least not during the day. Regardless, the roar of the surf thunders in my blood, and it fills me with joy.

Kyri must feel the ocean, too, although it fills him with something else altogether, defender of the realm that he is. (He's named after a royal character in *The MoonQuest*.) When we detour down a side street off the main drag to get closer to the water, he barks maniacally at the waves. Clearly, he's trying to scare them off and save Laguna Beach from certain destruction by tsunami. It isn't only monster waves that set him off. He barked no less fiercely at the tiny wavelets on the Clearwater River at Nez Perce National Historic Park in Idaho back in May.

Despite the summer crowds and Kyri's barking, a sort of peace washes over me. Whatever Laguna Beach is to me in the medium- or long-term, right now it's a welcome restorative after more than thirty days' journeying…and after this morning's panic.

As I wove through Irvine streets on my way here this morning, a monkey-mind chorus of doubts again questioned the wisdom of even considering making Southern California home. What was I thinking? If I couldn't make it in Portland, how could I ever expect to make it here? Considering it even for a nanosecond had to be a futile waste of time.

Then, from the random selection of music streaming into the car from my phone came these two songs: "Home I'll Be" by Nova Scotia's Rita MacNeil and Peter, Paul and Mary singing the Woody Guthrie classic, "This Land Is Your Land." When the final "this land was made for you and me" faded away, so did my anxiety and second-guessing.

Bottom line? Whether or not Southern California is or ever will be home, home I *will* be. Somewhere, sometime. I have to believe that, or how can I keep going?

Starbucks, Newport Coast, California
MID-AFTERNOON

This Starbucks in the Crystal Cove Shopping Center in the Newport

Coast section of Newport Beach (and a few minutes up Pacific Coast Highway from Laguna Beach) is one of my favorite cafes anywhere to write in. I discovered it during my ten-week sojourn in Southern California in 2010 and have returned to it whenever I'm in the area.

Here in 2010, I worked on early drafts of *The StarQuest* and *Acts of Surrender*. In 2017, I wrote the opening scenes of a still-untitled fourth book in my *Sara Stories* series here.

This is also where I once experienced a weird, small-world synchronicity. While waiting for my coffee one morning, I struck up a conversation with a woman who was waiting for hers. It turned out that a gallery owner I had recently met in Santa Fe was her brother. To top it off, she and her friend each bought a copy of *The Voice of the Muse* from me.

This Starbucks also has a great dog-friendly patio, with a Pacific vista that extends to the horizon out front and, out back, views up the slope toward sprawling, drool-worthy mini-mansions.

Once I'm settled with my signature Americano (two ristretto shots/one regular, topped with extra-hot steamed 2%), I pull out my iPad. This is the perfect day and place to return to work on my *Q'ntana* screenplay.

What makes the moment and setting even more perfect is when I overhear snatches of conversation from the two women sitting behind me. "I'm where my soul needs to be," one of them says.

Me too.

Day 37

Wednesday, July 3
Irvine, California

PREDAWN

This Independence Day week I'm doing my best to ignore the false patriotism and self-serving insanity coming out of the White House and to focus instead on what it means to me to be spending my first 4th of July as a US citizen.

On this day twenty-two years ago, two weeks into that first Fool's Journey road trip, I was camping at Sleeping Giant Provincial Park near Thunder Bay, Ontario, unaware that six days later I would cross the US border, for good. As I lay in my tent that night, Roxy in her favorite spot at my feet inside my sleeping bag, I could never have imagined how much my life would change as a result. I certainly never imagined that I would ever become a US citizen, a gift this country gave me on January 3 of this year.

There is much for me to contemplate, reflect upon and be grateful for this week, just as there is much to be concerned and anxious about — in my life and in the life of my adopted country. Yet I remain hopeful in both instances, even as it sometimes feels, in both instances, as though there's little cause to be hopeful. However, even in the middle of a sleepless night, I endeavor to remain optimistic that we both will emerge from these trying times stronger, lighter and brighter.

Beverly Hills, California
AFTERNOON

When I exited the 405 a few minutes after noon today into the jangled, manic chaos that is Santa Monica Boulevard, I thought, "This is insane. Maybe I felt called here to bring my thoughts and dreams about LA to some sort of completion. Why would I ever want to live here?"

I inched east into Beverly Hills through the traffic and turned off onto North Linden Drive, by the linear park that borders Santa Monica Boulevard in this part of town. My plan was to find a park bench, have my lunch and decide how to spend my afternoon in the city.

As I parked and stepped out of the car, two things happened.

First, the sun came out. Until then, the day had been gloomy and gray. Now, all was vivid and vibrant. It was as though the sun had been waiting until I set foot in Beverly Hills to burst through the clouds.

Moments later, I ran into a resident walking his dog. In marked contrast to all the dog walkers I had encountered in Laguna Beach, this gentleman not only smiled and said hello, he encouraged his dog to play with Kyri. The two pups got along famously, he and I had a pleasant conversation, and I walked away from the interchange feeling, again, as though the city was welcoming me.

Will I return here to live? That's up to the cosmic bankers. If they cough up the requisite finances, I would love to make this my landing spot...if not today, then sometime in the future.

For now, though, my Fool's Journey wanderings are set to resume on Friday, with another leap of faith into the unknown. Where to? Ask me again on Friday. How will it be funded? As it has been thus far: somehow, from one day to the next.

Day 39

Friday, July 5
St. George, Utah

LATE AFTERNOON

I spent my final SoCal afternoon yesterday back at the Newport Coast Starbucks that has been the source of so much creative inspiration for me over the years, happily at work on the as-yet-untitled fourth screenplay in my *Legend of Q'ntana* fantasy series. Now and again, I glanced up the hill to the pricey, ocean-view homes behind the shopping center and fantasized about gazing out to sea from my perfectly appointed writing studio in one of them. Then I returned my attention to the only view that matters — the words on my screen, *my* words — and got on with the story.

EVENING

As I pulled out of the Starbucks nearest my hotel this morning on my way out of town, the road I turned onto was Odyssey. Not Odyssey Road or Odyssey Avenue or Odyssey Street or Odyssey Boulevard. Just plain Odyssey.

To me, that was confirmation that it was right to leave and that my odyssey was meant to continue, at least for the time being.

It saddens me that the odyssey has directed me out of Southern California. But I'm counting on the opportunities, circumstances and resources (financial and/or otherwise) to show up that will make it possible for me to return and, if it's in my highest good, to stay.

LATE EVENING

This evening's 7.1 magnitude earthquake in south-central California missed me. Or, rather, I missed it. By the time it hit, I was already safely installed in my St. George hotel room.

Not that I'm ever anxious about earthquakes, fires, floods or other disasters, natural or otherwise. On each of these open-ended journeys, I have always traveled where Spirit (i.e., my intuition, gut, wisest self) has guided me, paying minimal attention to weather forecasts or other environmental indicators. And every time something potentially cataclysmic has occurred in my general vicinity, I have either been gone from the area before it happens, like yesterday, or I have arrived once all danger has passed.

In 1997, for example, I pulled into Fargo, North Dakota after an historic flood saw the Red River crest at an unprecedented fifty-four feet, sweeping away mature trees as well as saplings. Similarly in January 2005, a devastating mudslide in California's Ventura County occurred a few days before I drove through there. On both occasions, I knew nothing about the disasters until I witnessed the destruction left in their wake.

It's helpful for to me to have this reminder of yet another way I'm always taken care of and kept safe — not only on the road, but in the rest of my life. It's foolish (not Fool-ish) to worry...which, too often alas, doesn't stop me.

Day 40

Saturday, July 6
St. George, Utah

MORNING

I had a dream last night that I was conducting an amateur choir in Beethoven's "Ode to Joy." When the piece ended, I felt more than joy; I felt triumph. The performance was far from perfect, but it was exhilarating. And when I woke up I still felt triumphant.

It makes no sense for me to feel triumphant. After all, I am roaming the country with no idea from one day to the next where I'm going or where I'll sleep, and with no home to return to. Nor do I know more than a few days out, if that, how I will manage to keep this unorthodox enterprise afloat.

Yet as I ease into my fortieth day, the miracles continue to show up to keep me going.

This journey has been the most profound exercise in faith and trust I have ever experienced, and I have experienced many. Somehow, and some days it's far from easy, I must found a way to trust my heart and intuition to lead me to where I need to be, send me the resources to get me there and keep me safe along the way.

How interesting (and validating) that as much as I longed to stay in the LA area yesterday morning, I felt certain I needed to leave… just in time to miss the Mojave earthquake that rattled the city.

The powerful call to live there hasn't dissipated. But, clearly, it isn't time. Even so, I take to heart that snatch of conversation I overheard at Starbucks on Tuesday: "I'm where my soul needs to be." In that moment, I felt that I was, too.

Was the feeling for that instant alone? Or will it play out in a more permanent way at some point? Who knows? All I know is that if I am to be true to myself and true to all that I have written and taught over the years, I must continue to do what I'm doing and live as I'm living. And I must continue to trust that if I follow my heart, go where I am guided to go and do what I'm guided to do, I will be okay, in every way that matters. More than okay.

As for today, the plan is to leave St. George and head vaguely north, perhaps back to Pyramid Lake to integrate all my Southern California experiences. If so, there is too much emptiness between here and there, with too few pet-friendly hotels along the way, to go directly.

One option would be to drive toward Salt Lake City, taking detours to meander through the national parks east of I-15. Alternatively, I could take a different route altogether...or head in a different direction altogether. My only certainty, once I'm ready to leave, will be in which direction to point the car. The rest will reveal itself en route...to wherever.

Day 41

Sunday, July 7
Elko, Nevada

AFTERNOON

Given how anxious I was about money this morning and how certain I was that I could never find a way to fulfill the Beverly Hills dream (fantasy?) that keeps showing up for me, I was grateful for this afternoon's two signs. Literal signs that were also *signs*.

"In a quarter of a mile," my phone intoned as I drove down Lake Avenue in Wells, Nevada (pop. 1,022) trying to find my way back onto I-80, "turn right onto Easy Street." *Easy Street!?* Of course, I stopped to take a quick pic of the street sign. And I turned right.

Once on I-80 and a few minutes out of Wells, I passed Exit 348 to...Beverly Hills (pop. 0, apart from the eponymous Beverly Hills Ranch campsite). I was driving, so I couldn't capture that sign in a photo. Still, I don't think I'll forget it anytime soon.

It's hard not to doubt myself on this journey. It's hard not to doubt the journey itself. But with signs (that are also *signs*) like these, it's hard not to trust.

Fernley, Nevada
LATE EVENING

Tomorrow, the final day of my sixth week on this Fool's Journey, I head back to Pyramid Lake just north of here, a place that has already called me to it twice before in recent weeks.

Although I didn't consciously plan it this way, every stop at

Pyramid Lake has fallen on a Monday, the close of another week on this odyssey — as tomorrow's will. Each visit has also felt like a portal, a consequential pivot point on this journey and in my life.

During my June 17 and June 25 times at the lake, I sang the kinds of toning that I used to do as a sound healer and I claimed the life my heart desires as clearly and forcefully as I knew how. After each of those experiences, that life always felt closer, even if outward appearances have yet to match those sensations.

As I wind down for the night, tomorrow morning's outing is feeling especially potent — not only in terms of what within me it will activate, but what it will reveal. It's pointless to try to predict what will happen, so I will crawl into bed, let Kyri burrow under the covers after me and leave any more thoughts about tomorrow until tomorrow…

Day 42

Monday, July 8
CORNING, CALIFORNIA

EVENING

I checked out of my Fernley hotel first thing this morning and followed the now-familiar road up to Pyramid Lake: across I-80 through Wadsworth, up NV-447 along the scrubby Truckee River valley toward Nixon, past the Pyramid Lake Fishway and off the road at the same gravel pull-out as on each of my two previous visits.

Once again, I was alone. Only a rare car traveling the two-lane blacktop behind me broke the solitude and the silence.

Soft-edged streaks of fleecy white hovered above the low hills across the lake, while the sky overhead was clear and unstained. The air was still, and barely a ripple broke the water's surface as I gazed northward, past Anaho Island and toward the distant mountain wilderness.

Outwardly, everything was much as it had been last month.

Inwardly, however, I felt a more powerful earthquake than the one that struck California a few days ago. I can't put words to the time I spent there, other than to say that it was among my most potent and profound spiritual experiences ever. It was as though every moment of this journey, perhaps every moment of my life, had been preparing me for the hour or so I spent there. I say it was an hour or so, but I have no idea how long it was. All I know is that as I was driving toward the lake, I felt as though I was being stripped bare. And as I drove off, however much later that was, I felt reborn.

Maybe it's now time to return to Mount Shasta…

Day 43

Tuesday, July 9
CORNING, CALIFORNIA

EVENING

I'm not a morning person. Having Kyri in my life may have forced me up and out earlier than I did before I adopted him, but I'm not at my best first thing in the day. I'm often at my worst first thing in the day. In fact, it doesn't matter what time I open my eyes from whatever realm I've traveled to in sleep, even if it's after a short nap. It can take me up to a few hours to reintegrate into the waking world.

Some people prone to depression and despair are at their worst between three and four in the morning. And although I sometimes have those, my most intense feelings of hopelessness are generally when I wake up.

I don't suffer from clinical depression and I don't wake up every morning in despair, yet it happens often enough that I now recognize the signs and, mostly, am able to wait out the negative feelings. I wonder some days whether low blood sugar contributes, because breakfast will usually dull or dissolve those feelings. But not always. And, again, the feelings can strike at other times as well...like mid-morning today on the drive up to Mount Shasta.

I have written here before about my panic and anxiety on this Fool's Journey. But I have done little more than refer to the stress without going more deeply into it. I can't do that today. Today, I must do more than gloss over what happened. Today, however reluctantly, I must share it with you. If I'm to chronicle this journey fully and Fool-ly, I have no choice.

As I mentioned early on, "Be Vulnerable" is both my "Rule" #3 for memoir-writing in *From Memory to Memoir* and Step #5 in *The Way of the Fool*. "There is nothing to hide," I write in *The Way of the Fool*. "There is nothing to hold back. There is only you and me in the unparalleled beauty of our perfectly imperfect humanity. There is only vulnerability. There is only the Way of the Fool."

I wasn't panicked about money or anxious about where or when I might finally land when I woke up this morning, and I was grateful for the relative ease with which I greeted the day. As usual, Kyri was eager to get outside. So I washed and dressed, then took him for a walk through a neighboring field.

This wasn't to be a journeying day. Instead, I would drive up to Mount Shasta, do my thing on the mountain, then return to Corning for the night. So once I'd eaten breakfast, packed up a picnic lunch and picked up a coffee for the road at the next-door Starbucks, I made my way out of the parking lot and onto I-5.

The road from Corning to Shasta Lake, about twenty minutes north of Redding, is fairly straight, with the gentlest of rises lifting you a touch over five hundred feet along its fifty-mile span. Then, a little past Shasta Lake, I-5 begins its winding, three-thousand-foot scenic ascent through the Trinity Mountains to Mount Shasta City and beyond.

This morning, as the road climbed through dramatic hairpins and switchbacks, my anxiety climbed with it. Like so much of my anxiety, it was nonspecific…a sort of existential angst. And on this morning it transcended my Fool's Journey to encompass the fullness of my life's journey.

The despair I felt was overwhelming. Nothing I could say or do would shake it. *I'm three months from my sixty-fifth birthday, and what have I accomplished? I may have written a bunch of books, but I'm still homeless. I'm still penniless. I still don't know where I'm going or why…or why I'm bothering to go on. For more of the same? What's the point…of any of it?*

In that instant, the road veered sharply to the right. Ahead of me, a flimsy guardrail was all that stood between me and a sheer drop into a jagged valley. Could I? Could I say, "Fuck it all," smash through the guardrail and...?

Not for the first time in a moment of bleakest hopelessness, two things stopped me: Kyri, who lay sleeping in his bed in the passenger seat next to me, and my daughter, thousands of miles away in her Chicago college apartment. I couldn't take an innocent animal's life simply to ease my emotional pain, and I couldn't burden my daughter with a parent's suicide.

Would I have acted without those two brakes on my black mood? Possibly not. But I do know that Kyri, in the year he has been in my life, has rescued me more than once, at least as effectively as I rescued him. And for all that I was physically absent for much of my daughter's growing up years, a story I tell in *Acts of Surrender*, I couldn't intentionally absent myself from her life like this, not in a way that would so scar her.

It was a different dog, Roxy, who snapped me out of my first serious thought of suicide...or at least the first that I remember.

It was January 1997. Still nearly three years away from parenthood, I was living on the outskirts of Penetanguishene, a small town at the southeastern tip of Georgian Bay, a massive Lake Huron inlet that's nearly as large as Lake Ontario. "I'm afraid of the emptiness," I wrote in my journal a few days into the new year. "I'm afraid it will devour me, destroy me, annihilate me. Emptiness is death."

What would happen if I took my life, I wondered that gloomy morning, not entirely academically. Who would notice? What would happen to Roxy?

As happened this morning, it was my concern over the fate of my dog that snapped me out of it.

By the time I pulled into the parking lot at Mount Shasta City Park and settled under a mature oak with my picnic lunch, the sense of futility had passed. What had triggered it? I didn't know and still don't. The sole takeaway for me is to remember for the inevitable next time that the feeling passed and that I was and am fine.

After the morning's drama, my drive up the mountain — again to Bunny Flat, still the farthest the road was open — was uneventful.

Not so, my time on the trail, where, once again through tonal sounds that transcended language and conscious understanding, I sang the song of my soul, the perfect postscript to yesterday's visit to Pyramid Lake.

This is the most difficult piece I've shared thus far from this journey, and I'm a bit shaky from the experience of freeing it onto the page. It's ironic in a way. The Roxy story is already in *Acts of Surrender*, and in that book and *Dialogues with the Divine* I have let myself be deeply vulnerable, sometimes scarily so. However, the most revealing stories in those two books were released into the world years after they occurred. This one is fresh, achingly so, leaving me feeling more vulnerable than I did with either of those books.

Yet that's the point of "Rule" #3 and Step #5, along with so much else that I've written and taught over the decades. "Walk the earth naked, clothed only in your truth," I wrote years ago in *Dialogues with the Divine*. It didn't occur to me back then that there were layers of nakedness, and that the stripping down and stripping away would never end.

Day 45

Thursday, July 11
Albany, Oregon

EARLY MORNING

After two days of intensely powerful experiences — emotional as well as spiritual — I spent yesterday in the healing, womb-like embrace of Oregon's Rogue River Valley and Umpqua National Forest. The thick, luxuriant greenery and rushing streams formed a welcome contrast to the still, empty desertscape of Pyramid Lake and sentinel pines of Mount Shasta.

However, yesterday's landscape was not entirely benign: I was driving through volcano country. We're not talking about extinct volcanoes. According to a 2018 U.S. Geological Survey report, four of Oregon's volcanoes pose a "very high threat" of dangerous eruption, including Crater Lake, which is only forty-three miles from where I stopped for lunch.

MORNING

The affirmation associated with Step #7 ("Take Risks") of *The Way of the Fool* reads: "I trust fully, surrender completely and risk all as I open to the voice of my heart and let it guide me along the Way of the Fool. And so it is."

Alarmingly (though not surprisingly), I find myself living that affirmation on this Fool's Journey.

I have already shed most of my belongings: I have nothing in storage or in a friend's garage, and there is a limit to what you can cram into a Prius, especially when you're traveling with a dog. Nor am I journeying with savings, roomy credit cards or anything resembling a regular income...or much of an occasional income.

I didn't think about it before I left Portland forty-five days ago, nor had it crossed my mind until last night, but I *have* risked all to follow the call of my heart onto and along this journey. I have nothing to fall back on or go back to if this doesn't work out, if this soul-directed pilgrimage through the wilderness doesn't lead me to some sort of promised land.

Of course, as with all spiritual odysseys, the promised land is not an endpoint. It's *every* point. Through more than six weeks and nearly ten thousand miles, I have been gifted with countless promised lands. I have experienced phenomenal personal and spiritual growth and been mightily inspired. I have visited and revisited places of spectacular beauty. I have been cheered on and supported financially by people I know only as pixels on a screen. And I have experienced the unconditional love of the best little furry companion ever.

At the same time, it has been hard not to ask where all these thousands of miles are carrying me and who I will be when I land. It has also been hard to trust the fragments of knowingness that have come to me offering answers to both those mysteries.

Even when the knowingness has come in more than fragments, it has not been easy to trust.

This week's two pilgrimages, for example — back to Pyramid Lake and Mount Shasta — confirmed my overwhelming intuitive sensing that my ultimate destination is Southern California; more than that, that I'm destined for far greater professional success there than I have ever known, not to mention a more than comfortable lifestyle. (At the same, I'm aware that Spirit can be a trickster and that my human translation of whatever energy I'm picking up might not be accurate.)

Then, there's my mind, too easily stuck in survival mode and constantly wondering how I can keep going beyond the next few days. It can't imagine how my Southern California fantasy could be anything other than fantasy, let alone imminently possible... even when *The Way of the Fool*'s Steps #10 and #11 — "Embrace the Magic" and "Embrace the Miracles" — continue to show up, not only in theory but in action.

Just yesterday, for instance, I persuaded Comcast to waive my final bill. Of course, my mind's response to that miracle is to say that a $17.35 gift from Comcast is a tiny drop in a giant ocean next to the scale of miracle required to land me in Southern California... or even keep me going into another week.

My wisest self counters that the universe does not concern itself with scale. A miracle is a miracle is a miracle. And magic, as I write in *The StarQuest*, "simply is."

The thing about magic and miracles is that, by definition, they live in a realm beyond the mind's limited ability to imagine. That's where the faith that underlies surrender comes in. Without that faith, surrender is impossible. Without some deep, inner certainty that magic and miracles not only exist but are available and accessible, one cannot open to the voice of the heart and follow the Way of the Fool.

If my faith were absolute and my surrender unconditional, this journey would likely be unnecessary. Yet in the perfect imperfection of my humanity, there are days when my faith is as shaky as a toddler's wooden-block tower: The slightest touch sends it tumbling. On those same days, my surrender is anything but unconditional as I vainly attempt to bargain my way into an acceptable outcome.

Whatever else this journey is for me — and it has been many things so far — it is about growing into the much-deepened faith that makes unconditional surrender not only more possible but inevitable. It is about trusting that each step I take and every mile I drive is carrying me deeper into a more perfect experience and expression of my heart's desire and soul's yearning for this time in my life...for this lifetime.

As I sat in meditation 6,950 feet up Mount Shasta on Tuesday, what came to me with absolute clarity was that I need to make my way back to the LA area by the end of July and that, once there, I need to plan to stay. My job, I was "told," was not to figure out the how. My job was to leave that to Magic and Miracles. My job was to surrender and commit. My job, as always, was to trust.

I have been doing my (imperfect) best to do all the above in the hours and days since. To my limited mind, it is unattainable. But the heart knows what the heart knows, and my job — in my life as in my writing — is to listen and follow...even if it means risking all.

As I pulled up to my spot at Pyramid Lake on Monday, I caught sight of a small wooden sign across the road that I had never noticed, though it must have been there on my previous visits. It read, "Believe."

Stanfield, Oregon
EVENING

I experienced my third departure from Portland today.

The first, of course, was on May 28 when I left the city with everything I owned jammed into the back of my Prius, uncertain where I was going or how long I would be on the road. After the ordeal of trying to fit my entire life into the car, then getting the hell out of town, I was more numb than anything else.

The second, as I wrote on June 24, was emotionally turbulent — mostly sadness and grief...not merely for Portland and my aborted life there but for the parts of me I had outgrown, old parts that could not enter whatever new life I was moving into through this journey.

When I drove through Portland today, to pick up my copies of *Acts of Surrender* from the Multnomah County Arts Center and empty my post office box, I expected it to be emotionally neutral, and it was, largely. But as I crossed the Broadway Bridge then got onto I-84 to head east out of the city, retracing my May 28 route, I experienced something unexpected: waves of gratitude. I was grateful to the city for the brief life it had given me and for all the experiences, joyful and challenging, through which I had grown so much and which had prepared me for this Fool's Journey, itself a preparation for the next leg of my life's journey.

I don't expect to be returning to Portland any time soon. Now that I have done my leaving and my grieving and have expressed my gratitude, I see no reason to go back.

It feels as though the Portland chapter of my life is finally complete and closed. It feels, too, as though I am freer to move into the next chapter, whatever that is and wherever it takes me.

As I wrote this morning, I'm feeling called to make my way back to the Los Angeles area by the end of the month…and to stay there. It's clear that there remains some journeying for me to do. It's also clear that this phase of my journeying is coming to an end.

For tonight, I'm in Stanfield, Oregon, having moved inland from the Columbia River. I expect to be heading back to Boise in the morning. I'm not sure what the itinerary will be from there but, as always, I will undertake to follow my heart, moment-to-moment and day-by-day, in trust that I will continue to be taken care of… through this journey and beyond.

Day 46

Friday, July 12
BOISE, IDAHO

LATE EVENING

Among the intuitive flashes that came to me at Mount Shasta on Tuesday was that I need to return to Sedona, after which it will be time to go back to Southern California.

As I have already noted here, Sedona was my first permanent stop in the United States twenty-two years ago, and it's a place where I have experienced more transformations and life changes than anywhere I have ever lived.

To share but one example, Sedona is where this gay man fell in love with a woman and married her, and where our daughter was conceived. My wife and I moved to Hawaii before our daughter was born, then moved back to Sedona three and a half years later, which is where the marriage ended two years after that, in 2004.

If you knew me back when I was doing my regular sound healing/activation teleconferences and live events, Sedona is also where those had their genesis. More specifically, my God Activations, as they were originally called, were birthed the day I climbed to the top of Pyramid Mountain.

Not surprisingly, because of my three recent outings to Nevada's Pyramid Lake, it is that pyramid-shaped mountain that seems to be calling me back to Sedona. Of all the places in the area I could explore, of all the trails I could hike and all the energy vortexes I could visit, only that rock formation is drawing me. So that is where I'm heading from here.

My plan is to hike Pyramid Mountain on Tuesday, the day of the full moon/lunar eclipse. I can't know what's waiting for me there. All I know is that Pyramid Mountain sparked a new and unexpected source of income for me that sustained me for several years. I could use one of those right about now, especially if I'm to make my way to Los Angeles from Sedona.

Initially, I wasn't certain I would have the resources to get me to Sedona, let alone keep me there for a day or so. Now, I think I can swing it. Just.

The last time I was in Sedona on my own was in 2010, en route back to Albuquerque from my ten-week stint in LA. In a strange full-circle sort of way, I now feel called to return there as I head back to California.

Speaking of full-circle things, Boise, where I'm spending the night tonight, was one of my stops on that 1997 road odyssey. It's also a place where I had one of the most moving metaphysical experiences of my life — in, of all places, the steam room of the Boise Shilo Inn. I tell the story in more detail in *Acts of Surrender*, but it was amidst the swirls of steam that I sensed a visitation from my father, who had died twenty-nine years earlier on that same day.

As for tomorrow, I will likely head down I-84 toward Salt Lake City, spending the night there before continuing on toward northern Arizona and Sedona. I can't imagine what Pyramid Mountain has in store for me this time. I'm excited to find out.

Day 48

Sunday, July 14
Salt Lake City, Utah

MORNING

A few weeks before I knew I would be leaving Portland, I watched a video of the 2017 London stage production of *42nd Street* on BroadwayHD, a Netflix-like streaming service for live theater.

On one level, *42nd Street* is a trivial bit of fluff based on the 1933 movie musical that featured Ruby Keeler as Peggy Sawyer, a starstruck chorus girl who ends up replacing a show's injured star. Yet as I watched the 2017 video, it felt not at all trivial.

Something about the show struck a chord, and I found myself not only watching it over and over but repeatedly listening to the cast recording, especially when I felt called to launch this Fool's Journey.

My obsession didn't end there. Once I left Portland and was on the road, I would play the recording in the car as I was driving — multiple times some days. And some evenings, I would stream bits of the BroadwayHD version in my hotel on my iPad.

Yet it wasn't until I found myself repeatedly drawn to one musical number that I understood the show's significance for me.

I don't remember if this is how it plays in the 1933 movie, but in the stage musical, Peggy Sawyer is fired when she bumps into the show's star, Dorothy Brock, during a rehearsal.

When it's learned that Brock is so badly injured that she can't go on, the producer is set to cancel the show...until one of the dancers convinces him that Peggy Sawyer is talented enough to take the star's place.

The problem? The firing has crushed Peggy's dream of a Broadway career, and she is already at the station, waiting for the train to return her to her small-town home.

"I'm sorry, Mr. Marsh," she tells the producer, when he finds her on the station platform. "Show business isn't for me. I'm going back to Allentown."

During the production number that follows, first the producer then the entire company try to persuade Peggy to change her mind. "Come on along and listen to the lullaby of Broadway," they sing and dance at her for the next five minutes.

When Peggy finally relents and shouts, "I'll do it!", my fearful mind also surrenders. In that instant, I know that I, too, must meet my destiny head on by following my heart toward the realization of my dreams.

The first surrender that *42nd Street* helped me with was to this road odyssey. I can't tell you how many times I played the cast recording while shutting down my Portland life and preparing for this Fool's Journey.

The most recent is my decision to follow my heart back to Southern California (by way of Sedona), even as that decision defies all mainstream logic. Maybe, just maybe, I have enough bits and pieces of cash, credit and hotel points to get me from Salt Lake City, where I am this morning, through Sedona on Tuesday and then on to LA. Maybe.

Yet as things stand in this moment, even if I can get there, I may have nothing when I arrive. Of course, that's in *this* moment. In the moment-to-moment, day-to-day existence I am being called to live, there is no moment other than this one. And if I am okay in this one, and I am, I have to trust that I will be okay in the moments to come...wherever those moments find me, and that includes LA.

How can I doubt, the fearless parts of me ask the fearful parts, when I have experienced so many miracles over these past six and a half weeks? When I left Portland, I doubted I could make it past fourteen days. Yet here I am, entering into my forty-eighth.

From the three hotels that forgot to charge me a pet fee to the

Facebook friend who gave me a bed for the night, two meals and leftovers for the road to the unexpected donations (the modest and the astoundingly generous) to countless other miracles, I have somehow managed to keep going because every time Peggy Sawyer shouts, "I'll do it!", I shout it with her.

Peggy Sawyer leaves Allentown, PA with big dreams and ambitious visions of a Broadway career. For an instant, those dreams and visions vanish. When they come back, bigger and brighter than anything she could ever have imagined for herself, she is so terrified that she tries to say no.

In 2010, convinced that LA was where I needed to be, I took a leap of faith. I sold everything I owned and headed west. That year's miracle was the new friend who offered to have me stay with him. Like Peggy Sawyer's dream, however, things didn't work out the way I had hoped, and I returned to Albuquerque after ten weeks.

This is more than a second chance. It's the chance to realize that dream at a scale I can barely imagine being possible...even as the risk of another failure seems overwhelmingly high.

(Of course, "failure" doesn't exist, and true success cannot be measured in material terms, something I address in *The Way of the Imperfect Fool: How to Bust the Addiction to Perfection That's Stifling Your Success...in 12½ Super-Simple Steps!* I didn't fail in 2010, although my mind doesn't always see it that way. Rather, I gained immeasurably, in countless ways.)

For Peggy Sawyer, the risk of failure is huge. She has thirty-six hours to learn Dorothy Brock's part...and perfect it. If she fails, she will close the show. Worse, she will destroy any possibility of a Broadway career.

It will take guts, lots of hard work and, yes, a miracle to realize her dream. She has the first ("I'll do it!"), she does the second and, in the end, she manifests the third.

I have the guts and have put in the hard work — inner and outer — and, fortunately, I have more than thirty-six hours in which to manifest my miracle (or miracles). But not much more. If I leave Sedona on Wednesday, I will arrive in LA some time on Thursday, ironically, the same day of the week that Peggy Sawyer's *Pretty Lady* is set to open on Broadway in *42nd Street*. Fortunately for me, I have many more hours until my Thursday than Peggy Sawyer does to hers.

I watched that scene again last night. All these weeks later, I can't get enough of it. I keep needing it to remind me that when I say "I'll do it!", when I surrender to the voice of my heart, when I agree to follow the path of my soul, anything is possible...even the seemingly impossible...perhaps especially the seemingly impossible.

So, barring a shift in my intuitive guidance or my interpretation of same, I will point my car toward Sedona (via St. George, Utah) this morning and from there to Southern California. And even though I'm at least as terrified as Peggy Sawyer was, I will do my best to trust in the unimaginable miracles that will make my dream a reality.

If Peggy Sawyer can do it, so can I.

Day 49

Monday, July 15
SEDONA, ARIZONA

EVENING

When I opened my eyes to a chilly September morning in a Mount Shasta campground twenty-two years ago, I knew without the slightest doubt that I needed to start making my way to Sedona, a town I knew practically nothing about.

Last week's summons was not nearly as dramatic. Nor did it follow a mystical evening of revelation around a campfire, as my 1997 version did. Yet it still occurred the day after a profound spiritual experience, this time at Pyramid Lake.

There was no urgency to that first call, and it took me four days of meandering along the back roads of California, Nevada, Utah and Arizona to get me to Flagstaff; I drove into Sedona the next morning. This time, it took seven days, landing me here late this afternoon, the final day of my seventh week on the road.

The déjà vu experiences kicked in even before I hit town. As I wound down the spectacularly scenic Oak Creek Canyon from Flagstaff, I couldn't help but remember that first time. As soon as the canyon's soaring cliffs brightened from gray to vermilion on that inaugural drive, the beauty nearly had me in tears. "I'll never be able to leave this place," I'd whispered.

This afternoon's descent was too familiar to elicit that kind of response. How many hundreds of times have I driven those awe-inspiring miles over the years? Even so, I was moved.

A few hours later, my ex-wife, who returned to Sedona two years ago, insisted that this is where I belong, that I need to stay. For all I trust her intuitive sensing, I can't agree. My intuition on this remains unequivocal. I returned to Sedona for one reason: to get myself to Pyramid Mountain, then move on.

Another déjà vu awaited me at my hotel. I had used reward points to book ahead into the Arroyo Pinon at the western edge of town, and when I checked in this afternoon, the place felt eerily familiar.

"Was this always the Arroyo Pinon?" I asked the young woman at the front desk.

"No," she replied. "It used to be Kokopelli Suites."

Of course. During my 2004-to-2007 road odyssey, I had stayed here a few times when it was Kokopelli Suites — in a twin room so my daughter could spend the night with me. I hadn't recognized it when I'd made my online booking the other day.

Back in my room, I rummaged through old photos on my laptop until I found the ones I had suddenly remembered: of my six-year-old daughter by the pool in her blue mermaid costume.

Like Kokopelli Suites, much has changed in Sedona since I last passed through in 2014. Yet enough hasn't that it's as though I never left.

One final déjà vu for today: I'm now back from dinner with Linda Shay and David Rosenthal. They were among the first Sedona people I met here in 1997, and it was Linda who officiated at my wedding less than a year later. I hadn't seen them in fifteen years.

As for tomorrow, my plan is to hike Pyramid Mountain, then walk the Chartres-style labyrinth in the church parking lot next to the hotel. After that? Back on the road, I suppose.

Day 50

Tuesday, July 16
SEDONA, ARIZONA

MORNING

As slow as I can be to get going first thing in the day, it's hard not to be a morning person when you're in the desert in mid-summer and you want to hike. That's what got me out of my hotel a few minutes after six this morning for the short trip to Pyramid Mountain. Too much later and it would have been too hot, especially for Kyri.

The drive down Upper Red Rock Loop Road from West State Route 89a, Sedona's main thoroughfare, is nearly as scenic as the one down Oak Creek Canyon. Here, as you wind down the side of Schuerman Mountain, the vistas are breathtaking, offering panoramic views of some of Sedona's most famous rock formations, among them Cathedral Rock, Airport Mesa, Courthouse Butte and, in the distance, Two Nuns. This is also a road I know intimately. I have lived near the bottom of Upper Red Rock Loop Road three times through my various Sedona ins and outs.

It's spring 2004. With my daughter and her mom away for the afternoon and Pyramid Mountain a ten-minute walk from our front door, it's time to explore this rock formation that has been calling to me for as long as I've lived in this neighborhood.

On this Sunday afternoon, I never find the trail. Instead, I scrabble straight up the mountain toward the summit, a notepad in my backpack and a cassette recorder in hand. Why the tape recorder? Since returning to Sedona from Hawaii two years ago, I have been getting "messages" on my morning walks. (Thirteen of those now make up my book *The Book of Messages: Writings Inspired by Melchizedek*.) Some might call it channeling; I prefer to call it guidance and inspiration from my wisest self. Regardless, life has been stressful of late, and I'm hoping for some reassurance.

What explodes out of me about a third of the way up the four-hundred-foot climb is an evangelical fervency that is at once alien and invigorating. The message? "Be the God that you are." What evolves from that in the next days, after I transcribe the recording and broadcast it to my email list, are the God Activation events that, within the year, will be supporting me on my thirty-three-month road trip.

In those days, I wasn't using my birth name, Mark David Gerson — either out in the world or legally. I was Aq'naton Ben-Isha Yoseyva, a spiritual name that had insisted itself on me in late 1997 and was a variant, I would learn soon after, of the Egyptian pharaoh Akhenaten. I continued to use the name until a few weeks after I left Sedona in the wake of my marriage break-up.

Akhenaten was a revolutionary monotheist who took on Egypt's powerful priestly class and decreed that the many gods of their Amenist tradition were now folded into a single god: Aten, the sun god. He also changed his name, from Amenhotep IV, and is believed to have been Nefertiti's husband and Tutankhamen's father.

Why am I telling you this? Because as Kyri and I hiked the Pyramid Mountain trail this morning, the message I kept getting was that I needed to reclaim the Aq'naton part of me and reintegrate that energy and essence into my life as it is now.

I'm not sure what that means in practical terms, other than that I needn't change my name again. At the same time, I feel the power and imperative of it and will do my best to open to whatever is being called of me, even if my conscious mind can't figure it out.

Isn't that what spiritual surrender is all about? Isn't that the ultimate Fool's Journey?

As for my immediate Fool's Journey, my pilgrimage to Pyramid Mountain mandated no next steps. So I'll pack, check out and see where the car wants to take me. Toward Southern California...?

Day 51

Wednesday, July 17
Kingman, Arizona

MORNING

This morning I feel like Moses must have felt when, after leading the Children of Israel through the desert, he is told by God that he won't be allowed to enter the Promised Land.

Although God has not denied me entry into California and although the LA area still tugs at me, I will likely be turning north out of Kingman in an hour, even though I'm only about fifty-five miles from the California state line.

It's not that I want to return to Oregon, and the intuitive voices that I have endeavored to heed for the past thirty years urge me to continue west along I-40 toward Southern California. But I don't see how I can, which is why I expect to exit I-40 before I get there.

When the call came to revisit Sedona "before returning to LA to stay," I had hoped Sedona would provide either a financial miracle or the clarity that would show me how to proceed. Preferably, both.

Yet although my time on Pyramid Mountain was powerful, neither it nor my labyrinth walk at the church next to my hotel offered any clues as to how I could make my way to Los Angeles and be anything but homeless.

If Portland bled me nearly dry, this Fool's Journey appears to have finished the job. I'm not even sure I can make it back to Oregon without a few nights' sleeping in the car. Why Oregon? Logic suggests that, once there, I might be eligible for social assistance, given that that's where I'm a legal resident.

It was tough to write that last sentence. I have spent the past three decades letting my intuition guide me, often in direct opposition to where logic would have me go and what logic would have me do.

Those intuitive choices and leaps of faith have brought me more gifts than I can possibly list here, including the gift of fatherhood. Many of those choices and leaps were not easy, yet the gifts always outweighed the cost. Always. And despite the frequent challenges, I was always taken care of. Somehow.

Perhaps if I could find a way to surrender to my biggest leap of faith to date and continue into California, the gifts would ultimately outweigh the costs in this instance as well. Perhaps a way would be found to provide me and Kyri with a way to live.

But I have reached a place where "perhaps" is not enough, where the countless miracles that have sustained me through the past fifty days can no longer stretch far enough to keep me going in the direction of my dreams.

Once I left Sedona yesterday, I spent much of the day in tears — despairing, frightened and angry. My worst moment came when I passed an animal shelter in Prescott, Arizona, and for the briefest of split seconds, wondered whether it would be best for Kyri if I were to find him a new home. I cried hardest at that.

Still, I tried to keep a spark of hope alive within me. Maybe, I thought, Kingman ("king man") would have some deeper symbolic meaning for me. Maybe a last-minute miracle of sufficient substance would show up for me there. Maybe this Fool would be shown a way to continue his journey.

So far, nothing.

The thing about a Fool's journey, of course, is that it's unpredictable. Perhaps I was never meant to be in LA. Perhaps the journeys into and out of Portland had a deeper purpose. I can't know that unless and until that purpose reveals itself.

All I know is that for the first time in more than thirty years, I'm convinced that my only option is to turn my back on the infinite wisdom of my heart and listen to the fearful urgings of my mind.

That saddens me more than I can say. I try not to let it make me feel a fraud for all I have written and taught over the years. It's hard not to.

I wasn't going to write any of this. I was going to get out of bed, walk Kyri, then pack up and go. Yet I needed the perspective that writing so often gives me. If I'm not at peace with my decision to turn my back on California, I guess I'm resigned to it.

Then, once having written this for me, I wasn't going to make it public. But I owe those who have supported me so heartily over the past fifty days an explanation as to why I don't expect to be posting anything more about this Fool's Journey after today.

Of course, the journey will continue, as it always does. But the Fool-ish element of it looks as though it will end when I turn north on US-93 instead of continuing west on I-40, which, barring a miracle (or miraculous surrender), now seems inevitable.

I'm not sure what more I will have to say, about anything, here or anywhere, for the next while, other than to thank you for believing in me and in this journey and for supporting me so generously — through your words, prayers and donations. They have meant more to me than I can ever possibly say or repay. Namaste.

Day 52

Thursday, July 18
TONOPAH, NEVADA

MORNING

I said yesterday that I would not be sharing any more updates from my journey. However, so many people have expressed concern over what I wrote that I can't not make it clear that I'm okay. I don't know how I will make through the next few days, but I'm okay.

If my finances remain shaky and my dreams no less elusive, I'm still standing and I'm still determined to go on, although I'm more scared than I would prefer to admit.

One thing I do know is that within the hour, I'll be hitting the road for the Reno area and, more than likely, an unexpected fourth stop at Pyramid Lake. Given where I find myself this morning (Tonopah, Nevada; look it up), Reno is on the way to pretty much anywhere I'm likely to go. And as I'm no longer certain where that is, I'm counting on another dose of Pyramid Lake to trigger some answers.

Something else I know: As I head northwest on US-6 and US-95 over the next few hours, I will use my drive time to explore my relationship with my dreams and to examine where my fears fit into the mix. I will also seek more insight and endeavor to be open to the fresh miracles, financial and otherwise, that will free me to keep this odyssey going, which now feels more important than ever.

Day 53

Friday, July 19
Donner Pass Rest Area, California — westbound I-80

AFTERNOON

I'm in California. I probably shouldn't start this piece by giving away the ending, but I'm counting on that opening to be intriguing enough to keep you reading.

When I left Kingman on Wednesday, having given up on California, my plan was to aim for Oregon and the possibility of social assistance. At worst, I figured, I could live out of my car, an impractical option in the sweltering Southwest heat.

My heart whispered "Southern California" as I accelerated onto I-40; my head screamed *"NOT POSSIBLE."* I would exit the freeway at US-93 and veer north toward Las Vegas and Reno, then cut across the northeastern corner of California into Oregon.

"Last chance," I heard as I prepared to pass into the exit lane. For a split second I hesitated. Then I made my turn.

Once off the freeway, I pulled into the first parking lot, a Chevron station. Had I made the right choice? Had I somehow betrayed myself by turning my back on my dreams? By going against everything I had written and taught over the years? By refusing to follow my heart?

It didn't matter. I couldn't do it. I pulled back onto the road and continued north.

Not five minutes later, I sensed something. My intuition was trying to push its way through my fear. Here's what I heard: *You know how when you veer off your GPS's suggested route, it recalculates a* new route based on your new location? That's what has just happened. Your LA dream has not died. You will now get there via a different route and timeline.* There was more: *For now, continue heading north toward Oregon, but you may not make it all the way there.* And this: *You will not be homeless. You may choose to sleep in your car at some point. If you do, it won't be because you have to.*

I was doubtful. If all these years of intuition had propelled me into this absolute financial disaster, why should I trust it now? I reserved judgment.

A few minutes later, I called a friend and left a voice mail. When I hung up, my streaming music came back on. I hadn't been paying close attention to it before now, but this I couldn't ignore: It played this exact lyric from *The Phantom of the Opera*: "Promise me that every word you say is true."

Indeed.

About twenty minutes later, another lyric caught my attention, from a different song: "Every word I say is true / This I promise you."

Oh?

Then my friend texted me. "Not LA," he said. "Not never, just not yet."

By bedtime, after a long, lunch-less drive through the stunningly-stark-but-too-blazingly-hot-to-stop-in Nevada desert, I felt better… and more trusting.

I would still continue on to Fernley after Tonopah. From there, I would return to Pyramid Lake for more answers. As for Friday, no clue.

Thursday got off to a hopeful start with an impromptu playdate for Kyri, who had spent most of our journey deprived of other canine company. For the first time since leaving Sedona, I felt optimistic.

My upbeat mood didn't last.

"How much would you need to get settled in LA?" a friend texted me.

"Good question," I texted back. "I'm so accustomed to barely getting by day-by-day that I haven't considered anything like that."

So I did think about it. And as I did, the dream seemed even more unattainable. Then I checked my bank account and the balances on my surviving credit cards. Once again, LA was no longer the issue. Survival was.

As I was getting ready to leave Sedona Tuesday morning, I sat on the floor by Kyri's food dish, trying to help him feel safe enough to eat. Although he has been eating most of his meals, the almost-daily upheaval as I pack up and prepare to load the car sometimes so stresses him that he won't. Fortunately, those instances are rare.

Suddenly, I burst into tears. Sedona had pushed me through another massive rebirth; this time in less than twenty-four hours. Now, as happens with every newborn, I was being thrust out into the world naked and with nothing. I was terrified.

Recalling that incident two days later in Tonopah, I was even more terrified, forgetting that all but the least fortunate of infants is immediately swaddled and fed. Leadenly, I loaded the car and headed out of town, north toward Fernley and Pyramid Lake.

Moments later, however, something phenomenal happened that changed everything.

If you've read *Dialogues with the Divine*, you know about the "inner dialogue" technique I have used over the years for journaling and inner guidance. I also teach versions of it in several of my books[1]. So I am accustomed to having "conversations" of sorts with my wisest self (aka my higher self, God, Spirit or my Muse)...but not like the ones I had as I left Tonopah. These were more than conversations. They were out-and-out counseling/coaching/energy-work sessions, all out loud with my eyes open while driving.

The processes I was taken through were new to me, at least to my conscious mind. And they were so powerful and effective that I expect to incorporate them into my client work.

How effective? By halfway to Fernley, I had received more donations, in number and total dollar value, than I had received on any single day since launching this journey. By that same point on the drive, I knew that my GPS, which I like to think stands for *"God*

---

1. *Dialogues with the Divine*, for example, includes a section titled "Dialogues with Your Divine," which is a guide to launching a conversation with *your* wisest self.

Positioning System," had successfully recalculated and that I would be heading for California after all, if via a different route.

What were the questions I was asked as I drove?

- *Are you ready to live the life of your dreams?*
- *Are you ready to live the life of your dreams, whatever it takes?*
- *Can you accept that you will never be abandoned and that you will always be taken care of, regardless of surface appearances?*

My initial answer to those and many other questions was "yes, of course." Yet when I dug deeper, I was distressed to discover that I couldn't give an absolute, unconditional yes — not to any single question. By the end of the process, however, I could — to all the questions.

I was also asked to state clearly and in detail what those dreams were, and then whether I was ready to live every one. Again, it took some work to get to an absolute, unconditional yes for each.

By the time I reached Pyramid Lake late yesterday afternoon, the tough inner work had been done. All that remained for me to do was to ask for the energy of that land that is so sacred to me to ground and anchor those shifts, to express my profound gratitude to the land and to take in as much as I could of the spirit of the place so that I could carry it with me as I continue this journey.

Have all my financial concerns been addressed? Hardly. But the shifts within me that triggered yesterday's financial flow stripped away enough fear and anxiety to free me to move forward on those dreams that I now claim to be fully and Fool-ly ready to live.

While I have certainly felt courageous taking great leaps of faith in the past, I have rarely felt fearless in those situations. Since yesterday's experiences, I have, mostly…at least so far.

Are those shifts so firmly rooted within me that I can now forget about them? I wish. I'm having to return to those questions multiple times a day and repeat the processes in order to keep getting that absolute, unconditional yes. But that is worlds beyond where I was yesterday morning.

So what's the plan?

Today, I'm on my way to the Bay Area, to my Hayward friends. They have invited me back, this time for a couple of nights. I need some stillness, some time not driving and some nurturing after the intensity of recent days.

From there, if nothing shifts, I will make my way south toward LA/Orange County and start looking for transitional accommodation while I continue to focus on magnetizing to me all that's required to move more fully into the life of my dreams.

Once there, I hope to get back to my *Q'ntana* script and to the other writing projects that have largely been on hold during my travels.

I can't wait!

Day 54

Saturday, July 20
HAYWARD, CALIFORNIA

MORNING

Good morning, California!

I was a bit shaky and fearful when I woke up this morning, thinking about all that is required if I'm to manifest my dream. If I let myself go there, it can all feel manifestly impossible.

Then I remembered that my job isn't to manifest anything. My job is to stay out of fear and keep moving forward in whatever directions my heart pulls me.

The technique that my wisest self introduced me to and guided me through on Thursday helps me manage the first part of that. Continuing to listen, trust and take those actions that my heart, not my fear, requires of me handles the second.

Right now, I am out walking Kyri, doing that first part. Once breakfast with my gracious and generous hosts is over, I will meditate and tune into the second.

So I repeat: Good morning, California! I have come home. (Speaking those last two sentences aloud makes me cry. I must be on the right track.)

AFTERNOON

Last night in a private message on Facebook, someone questioned my integrity in seeking donations for this journey. It wasn't the first criticism I've received; they've been trickling in almost since the beginning. Early on, another private message accused me of being a "freeloader." But this was the first direct attack on my integrity.

Here's how I replied: "In a sense, it's like paying for a book only if you like it and you gain something from it. Or, put another way, it's like paying for therapy after it has helped you, not in advance. In other words, I'm making it possible for those who feel they're getting value out of what I am writing to 'give back.'"

I'm grateful that the messages of support I receive far outnumber the flak. I'm also grateful for the flak...even though it triggers my insecurity...*because* it triggers my insecurity. Criticism, even attacks on my integrity, force me to trust my intuition and inner knowingness and to continue letting myself be vulnerable, not merely by sharing my pain and my fear but by asking for help. Frankly, I doubt that I could have made it through these fifty-four days on the road had I clung to what was left of my stubborn independence.

There's another kind of private message that puts my trust to the test. This type is supportive, offering me intuitive insights about where it would serve my highest good to go and what it would be in my highest good to do. I got one of those earlier today. It directed me to Tucson. Others have pointed me to, among other places, Santa Fe, Boulder, Ashland, Austin, the Oregon coast and all the way up into Canada.

Part of me sure wishes I could accept any one of those sensings as gospel. What a relief it would be to rely on someone else for the certainty that so often eludes me. Mind you, how much certainty or accuracy can there be when each intuitive conclusion points me toward a different destination?

Still, with each suggestion, as with each criticism, I check in within myself and attempt to stay centered and anchored in what I know to be right for me in the moment, despite the many temptations to do otherwise. And that's the most important gift of those intuitive insights: They force me to stay grounded in my power and knowingness, which is a recurring theme of this Fool's Journey of mine.

Today, despite others' suggestions to the contrary, my intuition is pointing me back to Southern California. So I'll be heading south when I leave here tomorrow. How will the necessary resources fall into place? The only way to be true to myself is to trust that they will.

The only way to be true to myself is to trust in what I know in my heart to be true.

Postscript: After I finished writing the above, I sat down to lunch and set my phone to shuffle through my music library. The first song that played? "Amazing Grace." Amazing grace, indeed.

Day 55

Sunday, July 21
Hayward, California

MORNING

I'm often asked on my travels whether this Fool's Journey has created a conflict between my heart and my mind. It's a great question, but I don't see any conflict. Rather, when faced with a decision, I try to determine which aspect of me is motivated by fear, which aspect is ultimately wiser, and which ought to be in charge, tempered, of course, by input from the other.

Clearly, none of us can function without a mind. I sure couldn't write any of this without one. At the same time, the greatest dreams and desires are achieved and the greatest advances are made when we take the leaps of faith that only the heart can direct, leaps at which the mind often recoils. It has certainly been true for me up to this point — in my writing and in my life.

I recognize that, to many, my approach may seem foolish and irresponsible. Frankly, there are moments when it feels that way to me, too. But I have, in large measure, lived my life that way since my mid-thirties, and it has always worked out. More than that, it has always worked out better than I could ever have imagined possible.

It's a constant tightrope walk, for sure. Yet scary as it can feel, I have never failed to reach the other side, safely. Miracles, large and small, have consistently appeared when I've most needed them. Consequently, I would be foolish indeed to think that they would stop appearing (although it can be challenging to keep that candle of faith burning).

Even if that was hard for me to believe a couple of days ago, I have to trust that the same will be true for me in this instance. Otherwise, everything I have written, taught and lived over the years is a lie.

Of course, the thing about leaps of faith is that each successive one is from a higher cliff with a mistier view, if any, of what lies below. They wouldn't be leaps of faith otherwise.

That means each leap requires more faith than the last, which can be terrifying, as you have read from a terrified me in recent days.

Now more than ever, my daily practice is to stay as grounded as I can in the present moment. And it *is* a practice.

Whenever I notice myself dropping into fear and doubt (which I did first thing this morning), I force myself to apply the process that came to me on the way out of Tonopah the other day to pull my myself back, not into faith but into certainty — that in my absolute readiness to live my dreams, those dreams will find me.

AFTERNOON

I'm sitting on my friend's back patio, enjoying my first moderate temperatures in over a week and grateful for the pause in my journey that is freeing me to work on my screenplay.

Until a few days ago, this new story in my *Legend of Q'ntana* fantasy series had no title. Then, while I was driving and with my mind on other things, one bubbled up into my conscious awareness: *The Bard of Bryn Doon*. I have no idea what that means in the context of the story, which I still know hardly anything about. But every title that has come to me this way has always proven itself by the time the book or screenplay is complete.

When *Sara's Year* and *The Emmeline Papers* showed up as book titles, for example, I had barely begun writing those novels. At the time, I thought I knew what the stories were about, and those titles fit perfectly. In both instances, however, it didn't take long for the stories to veer off in unexpected directions, leaving me doubtful about the titles' suitability. For all my doubts as I moved through each story's first draft, the titles turned out to be perfect.

All this reconfirms what I've said all along: My stories are smarter than I am…the ones I'm living as much as the ones I'm writing. And as challenging as that can be to trust, especially on this journey, what choice do I have?

Speaking of this journey, I'll be hitting the road in the morning…in whatever direction the story chooses to take me.

Day 57

Tuesday, July 23
Arroyo Grande, California

MOMENTS PAST MIDNIGHT

I have spent my life coming out of hiding. Each day, each step, each breath has been a journey out of the shadows of perceived safety and into the open air of vulnerability.

It's a journey that has been going on since the womb; longer, perhaps, if you believe in soul choices and past lives.

If you've read *Acts of Surrender*, you'll know that a few months after my mother died, I learned that the man I thought to have been my father wasn't. In a house of secrets, it was a secret she shared only with her closest friend, who, once all the principals had died, shared it with me.

From conception through birth, I absorbed my mother's fear that I would be born resembling the wrong man. Thus, I developed my own fear, that it was unsafe to be who I was out in the world...that it was potentially unsafe to be seen.

I was born into hiding.

As a young child, I loved to hide from the world. Two favorite spots in our living room were behind the Dumont console TV that sat in the corner and, when we had company, behind the larger of the room's two armchairs.

Two long-ago snapshots also reveal my early discomfort with being seen: In one, I'm standing at the far end of the backyard at the entrance to a fort-like structure built of cardboard, looking fearful outside my sanctuary. In another, taken the morning of my first day of school, I am standing with my back pressed against the bricked-up corner of our front porch with that same frightened look on my face.

For the next decades and in many ways, I did my best to not let myself be seen, even as my wisest self kept pushing me out of one closet after another after another. Through that time, I always tried to fit in, tried to find a place where I felt I belonged, even as that same wisest self continued to demonstrate the futility of that quest.

When I finally started writing, something I never consciously thought I would want to do, my earliest creations were from my head not my heart and, for the most part, reached only small, specialized audiences.

Once I opened more fully to my creativity and increasingly allowed myself to become vulnerable in my writing, my readership stayed small. A modest cadre of loyal readers kept me largely safe from the hurtful comments and negative reviews that a larger audience might produce.

The same was true of my classes, workshops and speaking gigs. I created and disseminated powerful, transformational, life-changing material…yet it reached relatively few.

Despite my work's impact on those it touched, for which I have always been grateful, I kept myself in some form of hiding by not letting my work reach its fullest potential…by not letting me reach my fullest potential. How could I when at some deep level I was desperately afraid of what reaching that potential might mean? At best, I feared it would open me to scrutiny and judgment; at worst, to a level of criticism that might destroy me.

Ironically, it was that same fear that, years ago, kept me from attending creative writing workshops. I avoided them because my caricatured view was that after you finished writing, you rose to read what you wrote, everyone ripped you and your work to shreds, and you slunk back into your seat in bloodied humiliation.

What has any of this to do with Day 57 of this Fool's Journey? How is it related to Southern California and to this imperative that keeps pushing me in its direction?

I realized this past weekend that whatever else it might be, the whole inner push to the LA area is a powerful push out of hiding. It's a push to let myself be seen. It's a push to let myself step out into the larger world in a way I have always claimed I wanted to, yet that at deeper levels never dared to. It's a push, as I put it in *Dialogues with the Divine*, to walk the earth naked clothed only in my truth, but to do it on a bigger stage and larger scale than I have ever had the courage to do...than I have ever been fearless enough to do.

Of course, it could be possible to do those things anywhere. For me, however, LA feels like the place where all that finally comes together...as though it's that city's energy that will support this expansion that has been building within me, unrealized and unexpressed, for so long.

I wrote a few days ago that my eighteen hours in Sedona last week felt like a rebirth. At the time, I didn't know what that meant, only that it terrified me.

Now, I think I do. It feels as though everything I have been working toward — at inner and outer levels over the decades — has led me to this moment, to a moment when I am finally ready to claim my destiny and live my dream. Not my ego mind's dream, which would likely keep me hiding in fear, but the dream of my words and of my work, the dream of my heart, the dream of my soul.

If I'm to live that dream, I have to move past my fear of scrutiny, judgment, criticism and worse — a fear that is justifiably heightened at this time in this country, in too many countries, when compassion, respect, civil discourse, common courtesy and common decency have too often by replaced by scorn, disdain, derision, venom and violence. Yet it is precisely at this time when the voices of authenticity need to speak...when the voices of heart-truth need to be heard.

It is precisely at this time that I need to be bold in ways I have never allowed myself to be, to be unconcerned with potential fallout and blowback, to be immune to criticism, and to be fearless in ways that have never before felt possible.

A few weeks ago, I was attempting to change lanes on some freeway somewhere and no cars would let me in. "That would never happen in Portland," I muttered. There, at least in my brief experience, drivers (and pretty much all Portlanders) are super-nice, so much so that, while I was living there, I jokingly referred to the city as "Canada-lite."

Suddenly, I understood why I'd had to wait until I lived in Portland to apply for US citizenship and why that act had felt so threatening to my identity and sense of self.

Among the stereotypes of Canadians is that we are "nice," that we are self-effacing and that we are always saying "sorry." The joke goes that if you bump into a Canadian, he will apologize as if it was his fault.

All stereotypes, of course, including the affectionate ones, are broadly drawn exaggerations that ignore other qualities.

Yet whether it's my Canadian-ness or some other innate aspect of my beingness, I have also tended to be "nice" and self-effacing and apologetic. I haven't always been nice for the sake of being nice. I've been nice to be liked. I've been self-effacing to not stand out (i.e., to remain hidden in the crowd). And I've been apologetic for both those reasons.

In that moment on that freeway, I recognized that by becoming a US citizen, I had shifted my identity to shed not my Canadian citizenship (which I still proudly carry) but to shed those stereotypes that, in my life, were disempowering me.

They were also keeping me in hiding.

And to do it in "Canada-lite" Portland carried extra potency for me. Perhaps that's ultimately why I had to move to Portland and leave it behind.

Since the powerful healings I gave myself on my drive to Fernley and Pyramid Lake on Thursday and have been repeating ever since, I have done more than declare myself ready to live my dreams. I have declared myself ready to live unapologetically large, not because I'm better than anyone else, but because I'm better than I have ever allowed myself to be. Better, stronger, more creative, more fearless and more forceful. For me, at least today, Southern California feels like the best place to express that and to grow more fully into that... to lift the veil from my face, to remove the mute from my voice, to get my light out from under its bushel, to walk the earth naked clothed only in my truth. To step more fully and Fool-ly into my power. Or maybe that's what Southern California represents, and I need to be there merely to soak up that energy and move on.

Either way, that is one of the things that this Fool's Journey, which has stripped me down to my essentials, has been about.

As I write this tonight, I am in Arroyo Grande, about 175 miles north of LA on the Central Coast. I don't know whether I'll make it to the city in the morning, but I will make it there. Nor do I know how I'll sustain myself when I get there, and whether my new empowerment will attract to me the resources that will free me to stay. Nor can I know whether it will be in my highest good to stay.

What I do know is that I have been reborn, just as I sensed in Sedona. It's not the terrifying nightmare it felt at the time. It's the gift of a lifetime. The gift of a life. I'm not only ready to dive more deeply into it, I'm excited, exhilarated and ecstatic at the thought of it. And grateful. Indescribably grateful.

Day 59

Thursday, July 25
STARBUCKS, NEWPORT COAST, CALIFORNIA

AFTERNOON

Nine years ago, the town of Ojai, about thirty miles inland from Santa Barbara, was my gateway to Los Angeles. It was at Meditation Mount in the hills east of town that I knew it was time to act on my longstanding dream to relocate to Southern California.

I was in LA, selling books and offering coaching mini-sessions at the Conscious Life Expo when one of my oldest friends called to say that he would be spending a few days in the city on his way back to Toronto, a timing that lined up perfectly with the end of the Expo.

Sander was eager to visit Ojai, and I was eager to share Meditation Mount with him; I had been introduced to the spiritual center and its sweetly serene grounds during my 2004-to-2007 travels.

"We drove up late in the afternoon," I write in *Acts of Surrender*, "and as we walked behind the main building toward the gardens and overlook, we spotted a young man sitting on a low wall, strumming a guitar. The sun setting behind him bathed the valley below in a coppery light and threw a radiant aura around his head. He looked up when he heard us approach, and his long, blond hair glinted in the golden glow of approaching dusk.

"'Can I play you one of my songs?' he asked.

"Startled but intrigued, we sat next to him and he resumed his strumming, crooning softly in a velvet voice: 'I said I wanted open spaces, now I'm tradin' them in / Some things are better found within / My heart is the only open space I need to live in.'

"As I listened to the lyrics of Erich Lenk's song, I knew that the desire for physical open space that had so defined my life since I left downtown Toronto in 1994 no longer mattered. What mattered was that I expand the open space in my heart to encompass the dense physical spaces I had so long avoided. What mattered was that I surrender to my heart's desire, however foreign it seemed in the moment.

"Even as I sensed all that deeper meaning, what I said, silently, was, 'Shit. It's time.'"

Time for California.

Six months later, having sold or gotten rid of everything I owned (not for the first or last time), I took the largest leap of faith I had to that point ever taken: I pointed my car west on I-40 and headed for Los Angeles.

The miracle that made it possible for me to take that leap of faith and what happened next are too complex to go into here (they're chronicled in *Acts of Surrender*). Suffice it to say that twelve weeks later I was back in Albuquerque, my California dream still alive, if, like me, somewhat battered.

I didn't consciously remember that Ojai/LA connection on Tuesday when I decided to make a detour to Ojai on my way to the city from Arroyo Grande. But as I was driving up the mountain from Carpinteria, Sander called out of the blue.

"Shit," I exclaimed again nearly a decade later, not silently this time. "Meditation Mount is my portal to LA!"

Once in Ojai, I drove straight through town to the rural drive that leads up to Meditation Mount, only to be confronted by a "closed" sign, the same one that had barred me from the site a few years earlier.

Confused, I parked at the foot of the road and meditated on what had brought me all the way up here for no apparent reason. Was the "closed" sign telling me that LA was no longer a priority? How could it be, given all I had experienced in recent days?

No, I sensed. *The dream is as alive as ever. But the time for meditating on mountaintops is over for you. It's time for you to get down and dirty in the world.* (Later, I learned that Meditation Mount had been seriously damaged during an area wildfire and had been closed for several years.)

When I started up the car to return to Ojai for a picnic lunch, the *42nd Street* overture blasted from the speakers, even though a track from a different album was queued up to play…another powerful urging to say yes to my dreams. Apparently, LA was still on. I simply needed to stay open to how it might be possible.

Irvine, California
EVENING

I had something of a shock when I went to check into my hotel last night: There was no reservation in my name, and the hotel was sold out.

No room at the inn.

It wasn't the hotel's fault. I'd mistakenly reserved for tonight and tomorrow, not for last night and tonight.

That wouldn't have been so bad had I not spent the previous two hours crawling through rush hour traffic to get from LA to Orange County. I was hot, tired and hungry, Kyri was restless, and the hotels that the front desk called for me were either sold out or didn't take pets.

When I launched this journey in May, I knew that Kyri wouldn't prevent me from doing anything or going anywhere that mattered. On the contrary, he would filter out all the things I didn't need to do, the places I didn't need to be and the hotels and motels it was best I not stay in.

I still believed it last night after nearly thirty minutes in the car, fruitlessly making calls and scouring websites and hotel apps. Were we going to have to sleep in the car after all?

No, as it turned out. I finally found a place in Anaheim, in the heart of Disney country. The good news? No pet fee and a room rate lower than I'd expected. The bad news? It was another twenty-five minutes away through rush hour traffic — twenty-five minutes to give my uncertainty plenty of time to flourish, twenty-five minutes to give my anxieties plenty of time to fester.

All kinds of what if's, none desirable, battled each other to get my attention. Was I insane to push myself to the edge for an elusive dream? Delusional? On the surface, my anxiety was about money. In truth, it was about more than that.

The deeper I have probed in recent days, the more I have come to understand that my fears are more often than not about the dream itself. Yes, money is a real, practical concern, especially in pricey Southern California. Yet money wasn't at the core of my anxiety last night. As I noted from Arroyo Grande the other day, it's about coming out of hiding, about "playing large" in the world, about letting myself be seen, about walking the earth naked clothed only in my truth.

That was no less true on the drive to Anaheim.

I'd had similar doubts on Tuesday when I was having a hard time finding an LA-area place to spend the night. Any hotel that was available and took pets was considerably more expensive than anywhere I had previously stayed. That was one of the reasons I chose to stay in Ojai that night.

Stressed, I called a friend on a similar spiritual path who usually gives me a powerful, tough-love pep talk. Unfortunately, he was also experiencing challenges that afternoon, and his fear-based advice did nothing to ease my anxiety. Instead, it stoked it.

After dinner that evening, no less shaken, I took Kyri for a walk into downtown Ojai. Leisurely walks are often meditative for me, and Tuesday night's was no exception. By the time I returned to my room, I was centered once more and largely at peace with my journey and my intuitive knowingness: I was to look for an LA room the following morning and be prepared to spend more for it. How could I expect to expand into my dream if I was busy contracting out of fear?

Of course, my intuitive knowingness didn't guide me to screw up my reservation. Nor did it stop my doubts from resurfacing on the drive to Anaheim. If I had arrived in Southern California to stay, as my intuition suggested, why was I heading for touristy/transient Disney country?

I had no immediate answer, and my evening walk with Kyri provided no further insight. I went to bed feeling more unsettled than I had felt in over a week. Why the hell was I in Anaheim, of all places? I couldn't figure it out.

I slept fitfully and woke the next morning no less distraught. The hotel's breakfast room, which echoed noisily with the excited chatter of kids impatient for their first Disneyland adventure, didn't help.

Or maybe it did.

"Jiminy Cricket," I exclaimed as I headed back to my room, recalling the beloved Disney character and his song, "When You Wish Upon a Star."

Anything my heart desires? No request is too extreme? Dreams do come true?

I wish I could say that the instant I repeated the lyrics, my mood and energy shifted. They didn't. It took a few more hours of conscious work, consciousness work and writing to neutralize the negativity and return me to myself.

Writing and the consciousness work involved in restoring and holding the highest vibration are all I feel called to do these days. And as writing for me is nearly always about restoring and holding the vibration, it's the most important thing I can be doing, regardless of conventionally practical considerations.

Conventionally practical considerations, my intuition tells me repeatedly, are irrelevant. The only way to live the dream is to live the vibration of the dream — as fully as I can. Everything else is a distraction.

It can be a struggle to leave my mind and the ways of the everyday world out of it. But the heart alone is wise, and the heart alone holds the vibration of the dream.

Holding that resonance (and restoring it the minute I notice it slipping), is a full-time job. It's also the hardest work I have ever done.

As for me and LA, I'm booked into my Irvine hotel until Saturday morning. Beyond that...? It will depend on what shows up in the meantime in terms of opportunities, financial resources or both.

I'm feeling guided to stick around. However, I'm prepared (more or less) to leave should that feel right. "Place" is an important part of the dream, but the dream is bigger than any single place. Wherever the dream takes me is where I will be.

Day 60

Friday, July 26
STARBUCKS, NEWPORT COAST, CALIFORNIA

AFTERNOON

What a difference a day makes. More to the point, what a difference eight words make.

I didn't know I was going to write "the dream is bigger than any single place" yesterday until the words typed themselves into my computer. But, then, there's hardly anything about any of my writing that I consciously plan. It comes as it comes and I hang on for the ride, much like this Fool's Journey I'm on, which clearly operates from a higher purpose and imperative than anything my conscious mind can discern or interpret.

My heart knows, however, and as long as I am able to stay connected with that higher wisdom, I know I'm on the right track, even if that track isn't always visible.

Which brings me back to those eight words and to the paragraph they sit in...

"I'm feeling guided to stick around [LA]," I wrote. "However, I'm prepared (more or less) to leave should that feel right. 'Place' is an important part of the dream, but the dream is bigger than any single place. Wherever the dream takes me is where I will be."

Those words stuck with me all night. Frankly, they shook me up. After all I had been through to get me here, including my panicked false start nine days ago, was I being called to leave?

That was the question I asked as I walked Kyri along Irvine's San Diego Creek trail this morning. The day was already steamy at

8:00 AM, and moving slowly was the only practical option. It was the perfect speed for a meditative stroll.

"What do I do tomorrow?" I asked. "Do I look into staying in the area, or is it time to move on?"

The answer I intuited surprised me.

By coming here in the belief that you had come to stay, you faced down some of your greatest fears. But the journey is not over. You may choose to return — to visit or to stay — but you have accomplished what you set out to accomplish, and you are stronger for it. It's time to move on.

There was more.

You are already living the dream, through your journeying and your chronicling of it. The dream is bigger than any single place, which is why the traveling must continue for a time. Not for a long time, but for a time.

I can't say whether I was disappointed or relieved. A bit of both, if I'm honest. I always feel so vibrant when I'm in LA. And the Newport Coast Starbucks where I am writing this and where I have written so much over the years is not only in a stunningly beautiful setting, but has always fed my creativity. At the same time, the resources and opportunities that would keep me here have yet to show up.

That alone wouldn't push me out. Had the call been for me to stay, a way would have been found.

The bottom line, though, is that it wasn't. So I will pack up the car tomorrow morning, and Day 61 of this Fool's Journey will carry me wherever I need to go next.

As I sit here on this patio gazing out toward the sea, I can't help but hope it will ultimately be back here. At the same time, I have to believe that wherever I am called to land will be perfect and that I will be fully supported to be there. It has always been so. Why should anything change now?

A postscript: When I returned from my meditative walk this morning, I found an email from PayPal alerting me to a donation that had come in from a coaching client. Generous though it was, it was the accompanying note that moved me to tears in its validation of my journey: "You are so different, Mark David. I've never known anyone who can step off a ledge like you can and trust there will be someone or something to catch you." A few minutes later, a stranger tagged me on Twitter in a meme that read, "Be you. The world will adjust."

Irvine, California
EVENING

As I turned away from the ocean and drove up Newport Coast Drive toward my hotel this afternoon, it saddened me to leave the area behind, possibly for good. Then I heard, "You'll be back."

A few minutes later, I turned off into a tiny park that has been empty nearly every time I've stopped by over the years: Los Trancos Canyon View Park. It sits high on a ridge overlooking the desert-y San Joaquin Hills and, beyond them, an endless Pacific vista. It played a pivotal role in my 2010 departure from the area, and if I am to return it was a fitting place from which to say au revoir...until we meet again.

Day 61

Saturday, July 27
Kingman, Arizona

EVENING

It's too early in the morning after a restless night during which I hear the song "Getting Out of Town" from the musical *42nd Street* playing in my head each time I wake up, which is often.

Were I to consider the song's context in the show, I might view it as something more than a confirmation of the call to leave LA. I might view it as confirmation of an eventual return. That's because in the musical, the cast of *Pretty Lady*, the show within the show, is leaving New York for Philadelphia. Assuming a successful run of out-of-town previews, cast and show will return to open in the big time, on Broadway.

As I lie in bed reluctant to face the day, I can't see the promised return suggested by the song. I'm no less wobbly a few hours later as I pack up, load the car, top up the gas tank, pick up my Starbucks and point the car toward Barstow and Kingman.

It doesn't matter that I heard "you'll be back" as I drove out of Newport yesterday afternoon. All that matters is that I finally found the courage to make my way to LA and now, less than seventy-two hours later, I've been pushed out. Again.

What am I to do? Where am I to go? As so often happened early on in this journey, I feel lost and purposeless. I try to connect with my wisest self, but there's too much static.

Finally, as I merge onto I-10 a while later, the static clears enough for me to hear this series of questions, a variation on those I have been asked frequently since the drive out of Tonopah what seems so many lifetimes ago…

- *Are you ready to live the life of your dreams? Whatever it takes?*
- *Are you ready to fully live your passion and realize the full potential of your spiritual purpose? What if that means you have to make yourself more vulnerable than you have, and to a larger public?*
- *Are you ready to come out of hiding and "be seen"? Are you ready to walk the earth naked, clothed only in your truth?*
- *Are you ready for the level of scrutiny and, perhaps, criticism and judgment that that level of visibility will inevitably bring?*
- *Are you ready to live your life under a microscope?*

I can truthfully answer yes to the early questions in the series; I can't to the later ones. Not truthfully.

This is tough. Way tougher than I ever thought it would be.

It doesn't matter that four days ago I committed to coming out of hiding and being seen. The implications of that commitment now plunge me into panic.

My chest tightens. My stomach knots up. My inner child screams, "If I reveal who I am, I won't be safe. I'll be destroyed."

Then I recall the fallout from what I posted on Facebook yesterday, about leaving LA. While masked in the guise of support, it was negative, critical, fear-based and judgmental, presuming to know more about my highest good than I do. And it didn't hesitate to tell me what I ought to do to "save" myself from certain doom.

I handle the first comment reasonably well, but the second and third — which show up once I'm on the road — make me physically ill, showing me just how ultrasensitive I can be to perceived scrutiny, criticism and judgment.

It's then I realize that I can't live the life I feel called to live as publicly and vulnerably as I feel called to live it if my stomach turns at the slightest criticism. I must be prepared to live my life under a microscope, and not shrink at whatever prodding and provocation might result.

Frankly, I have to toughen up.

At the same time, I must keep my heart open and stay vulnerable in my life and in my work. I have to be ready to walk the earth naked clothed only in my truth, and I have to be prepared to deal with the consequences.

Only then do I grasp why I had to leave LA this morning and why I had to make my departure public. If I hadn't, I wouldn't have attracted the criticism that so triggered me, nor would I have uncovered this core issue that must be addressed before the life of my dreams can be possible.

I *had* to leave LA when and how I did, and the criticism, as challenging as it was, was a huge gift.

What's next? And where?

I get to work with that core issue over the next days. Writing this is part of that. Writing is not only how I communicate and teach, it is one of the key ways I meditate, process, do my inner work and grow.

As for tomorrow, I don't know where I'm going. It probably won't be back to LA. Not yet. I'm not a hundred percent ready for that dream. I'm getting there, but I still have a distance to travel.

At a physical level, I have been traveling that distance through the intense heat of the Mojave Desert. It was 119 degrees Fahrenheit at one point during the drive here, and it reminded me of a story a Facebook friend shared with me recently.

She told me of a road trip a while back that kept carrying her to places where there were fires. In the end, she perceived that she had been on a journey of purification. As the phoenix experiences, sometimes the old must be burned away before the new can emerge.

I encountered no fires today, but with such searing temperatures, I may be experiencing my own journey of purification through the fiery desert heat.

The desert is symbolically significant in another way: To reach the Promised Land, the Children of Israel spend forty years wandering through the desert. Fortunately, we live in accelerated times and with any luck, I will be able to squeeze my wandering into a couple of days and land once again in my promised land, this time for longer than seventy-two hours.

I'm profoundly grateful to all those who have supported me and cheered me on, as well as to those who have shared with me how my journey continues to inspire them on theirs.

I'm equally grateful for the judgment and criticism. It forces me to remain centered in what I know in my heart to be true, and it strengthens me for the journey ahead. It, too, is a gift.

Day 62

Sunday, July 28
FLAGSTAFF, ARIZONA

LATE EVENING

At the end of the afternoon today, having taken a scenic, off-freeway detour through Prescott to have coffee with an old friend then drive through Sedona without stopping (a first), I parked at a vista point at the top of Oak Creek Canyon. Between the overlook and the Indian Market, this is a popular tourist destination, and as I wove through scores of visitors I started thinking about the whole "under the microscope" thing. "How would it feel," I asked myself, "to be so recognizable that it would be a challenge to be out in public in a place like this without being stopped?" I had barely finished formulating the question when I was stung by a giant wasp. (I haven't been stung by a wasp since I was eleven or twelve and, fortunately, I'm not allergic.)

In the hours since, I have been contemplating the meaning of the incident. Normally, I would go online to look up what wasps represent in various traditions. Today, however, the sting's timing felt more significant. After all, the instant I asked what celebrity would be like, I was stung.

Here's what I have come up with: The sting was to remind me that the dream doesn't come without its drawbacks, even its pain. At the same time, I was never in any danger, the immediate pain subsided within minutes and all that remains is a dull ache that is certain to be gone by morning. However the dream plays out, the wasp sting assures me that I will be fine.

♪ ♪ ♪ ♪ ♪

I wasn't going to share anything about my day today, including the wasp incident, until it struck me that my reluctance was directly related to what I wrote last night about letting myself be vulnerable and about being tough enough to withstand any fallout.

I wasn't feeling tough this evening, though. In fact, without realizing it, I had shut down. At some unconscious level, I had determined that it was safer to keep my mouth shut. Instead of walking the earth naked, clothed only in my truth, I had donned a suit of chain mail and covered it over with armor. If I kept silent, my frightened child-self determined, I would be safe.

Yet this path I have been called to isn't about safety; it's about risk. It isn't about hiding; it's about being seen. It isn't about playing small; it's about living large.

It isn't about silence.

I can't remain silent. I can't remain silent and be the writer I am. I can't remain silent and be the teacher I am. I can't remain silent and live my authenticity. I can't remain silent and expect the dream I am journeying toward to manifest.

If I remain silent, there is no dream.

The vision I have for myself is big, so big that it feels egotistical to share it. Except that if my ego mind were in charge, there would be no dream. My ego mind is terrified of the dream. My ego mind would prefer the monastic life of a scribe in retreat, far from the perceived dangers of the world.

The problem with that is that the writer's fear infects the writer's words, circumscribing their reach, limiting their impact and depriving them of *their* dream. For it is the words' dream that feeds the writer's dream, unless the writer is too frightened to free that dream into the light.

My dream is that my books and movies do more than change the handful of hearts and minds they now affect so powerfully. My dream is that they change the world. Perhaps the scale and scope of that dream is why I feel so powerfully called to LA, not because the city can necessarily make the dream happen, but because a big dream requires big energy painted onto a big canvas. Few energies and canvases in this country are bigger than LA's.

I know the dream is possible. I know it with every fiber of my being. I also know that the only thing preventing my words and stories from having that kind of impact is me. At the same time, the only thing that can free that dream to manifest is me, which brings me to how I spent my day.

Much as I did yesterday, I worked with the issues I need to resolve — if not perfectly, then enough to fuel the dream. There were moments when I could answer yes to today's version of yesterday's questions with certainty and confidence, and there were moments when I could not. As I noted here a few days ago, it's a practice in "holding the vibration and resonance." That's a moment-to-moment practice.

So, here's the big question: Am I ready to return to LA? Perhaps the real question is, can I trust myself to hold the vibration and resonance consistently enough to give the dream a chance? I have no answer. I'll ask again in the morning — after I check out, top up my tank and pick up my Starbucks. So often on this Fool's Journey, it is only then that I am able to intuit my next direction.

Day 63

Monday, July 29
Tustin / Santa Ana, California

LATE AFTERNOON

It's five in the morning. The first hints of daylight are poking through my Flagstaff hotel's blackout curtains, and I'm in a panic.

Is it really time to turn around and return to California? I just left two mornings ago. Or am I delusional?

I have been at this Fool's Journey for nine weeks now, and what do I have to show for it apart from having clocked seventeen thousand miles? Am I any nearer to this "life of my dreams"? Or will it ever be anything more than a dream?

If I'm honest, what is stressing me now is California and the promise it represents…if that is what it represents. That's how much doubt I'm in this morning.

"Well, if I am to start heading back to California today, at least I can stop for the night in Kingman," I soothe myself by saying. Then I check the map on my phone and see that Kingman is only two hours away.

Barstow, then. I check the map again; Barstow is only two hours from where I have previously stayed in Orange County.

If I'm going to go, I guess it makes the most sense to go all the way, though it's a seven-hour drive, longer than I prefer to be on the road and a long stretch with a dog.

I'll decide later, I say, and try to get back to sleep. My frightened, overactive mind won't let me. A few games of iPhone backgammon still the voices but not the panic. Sleep continues to elude me.

Finally, I roll out of bed, get washed and dressed and take Kyri for his walk.

I know that first thing in the morning is never my best time. Even as my mind continues to drown in doubt, I'm certain that my anxiety will subside and that I will somehow get on with my day, wherever it takes me. Deep down I know, too, that these sixty-something days have not been a waste, that I have grown hugely during that time, that I truly am nearer to the life of my dreams. Yet it's hard to drill down that deep at this hour.

By the time I have had breakfast, packed, loaded the car, topped up the gas tank, picked up a few groceries and collected the nearly always compulsory Starbucks Americano, I have decided to drive straight through, despite some lingering queasiness. And after a picnic lunch in a sweltering, somewhat ripe-smelling Kingman dog park, I book three nights near Orange County's John Wayne Airport.

The rest of the drive is largely uneventful, apart from another Facebook comment that offers me an opportunity to stay grounded in what I know to be true and a joyful if unexpected reunion with a good friend I haven't seen in three years. When we arrive in Barstow from different directions within ten minutes of each other, I have to concede that the universe must be in perfect alignment and all must be well.

Yet a small subset of my morning doubt resurfaces when I get to my hotel two hours later. Unlike the quiet, almost oasis-like setting of my previous Orange County hotel, which adjoined a nature trail and was walking distance from a park, this one sits at the intersection of two multi-lane thoroughfares. In a sense, it's a perfect metaphor for my leap from the retreat of my previous life into the busyness of Southern California. Knowing that makes it no less jarring.

So, I'm here. The goal (and current guidance) is to stay…although I'm not sure what that means, apart from the two tasks requiring my nearly immediate attention: Kyri's annual shots and my car's thirty-thousand-mile servicing.

I'm not certain how I will pay for either, although I'm sure I will manage, somehow. I'm trying to be equally doubt-free about how I'll manage to stay in Southern California, especially when I feel called to take no direct practical action to "make it happen." All I hear is, "Do your inner work and write, and make space for miracles." That could change in the morning, of course, but that is the truth of the moment.

For now, I'm simply grateful to be here. As for tomorrow and beyond? They will take care of themselves in their time, as they always do. I have to believe that or I can't keep going.

EVENING

I mentioned this afternoon that my hotel sits at the intersection of two busy streets. What I hadn't noticed until I went for a walk after dinner was that across one of those streets is a park and the new Flight at Tustin Legacy development, named for the two massive blimp hangars built nearby in 1942 to house the US Navy's World War II Airship Patrol Squadron.

Rising seventeen stories high and extending more than a thousand feet in length and three hundred in width, the hangars are still two of the largest wooden structures ever built...truly larger than life. And across the park from the hotel, a dirigible-themed mural highlighting seven people in a balloon basket, drinks in hand, suggests how easy it can be to take off in flight.

As well, my hotel sits on the border between the Orange County cities of Tustin and Santa Ana. Thanks to a little online research, I have discovered that "Tustin" is a form of Thor, mostly known as the Scandinavian god of war. Turns out he's also the god of fertility, which could as easily relate to creative output as to fecundity. And Santa Ana? St. Anne was the grandmother of Jesus, but the name Ana comes from Hebrew and Latin words meaning "grace."

Flight, fertility and grace...all larger than life: Maybe I *am* in the right place after all.

Day 64

Tuesday, July 30
STARBUCKS, NEWPORT COAST, CALIFORNIA

AFTERNOON

Another dawn, another panic. It's Tuesday, the first day of my tenth week on this Fool's Journey and my first full (Fool?) day in Southern California. More accurately, it's my *third* first full day. I've already had two "dress rehearsals" in the area, and I'm doing my shaky best to view this one as the opening night of a long, successful run.

I wake with two songs playing in my head. One is a wedding song: "Beautiful in White" popularized by Irish pop singer Shane Filan; it's hard to know what to make of that one. The other's meaning is more obvious, at least potentially: "The Impossible Dream" from the musical *The Man of La Mancha*.

I find a music video of Il Divo performing the song live in Japan, and about halfway through I burst into tears...although I can't be certain whether I'm crying because I'm feeling ennobled or because I'm afraid the song is warning me that I'm engaged in a quest that's doomed to futility.

The day's mood suggests the latter. I spend the morning and part of the afternoon meeting a deadline related to my Oregon Medicaid, a tedious exercise in accounting that is anything but ennobling. Should I remain in California, it may also prove to have been an exercise in futility.

Now that I'm here, allegedly to stay, I'm not sure what to do with myself. If I were a normal person, I would focus on finding a less transient place to live and seeking a way to support myself. At the very least, I would research veterinary clinics for Kyri's annual shots and Toyota dealerships for my car's servicing.

I'm not a normal person. If I were, there would be no Fool's Journey and I would never have left Portland...or Albuquerque...or Sedona...or Toronto...or Montreal. I certainly wouldn't be sitting in a Newport Coast Starbucks, writing.

Yet that's precisely what the call is, at least for this afternoon.

I don't have the resources to go home-hunting, although that wouldn't stop me if that's what I felt called to do. Kyri doesn't need his shots for another ten days, so there's no urgency to act. My car is due for an oil change, but it can wait another few thousand miles before that servicing becomes critical.

As for supporting myself, I *am* supported, if not in ways that make me particularly comfortable. I'm booked into a cozy extended-stay studio for two more nights, and that's plenty of time for worlds' worth of miracles to reveal themselves.

And I'm writing, which is at the core of the "life of my dreams" and is the sole activity that feels right in this moment (as in many moments). And in this moment I'm "living" in Southern California as I do it.

The key phrase in all of that is "in this moment."

In this moment, everything is not only good, it's better than good. In this moment, there is nothing to worry about, for all worry removes me from this moment. In this moment, I am sitting in an astoundingly beautiful place. I am writing, which nearly always restores my energy and vibration (neither of which were great when I sat down a few hours ago). And if I am *The Man of La Mancha*'s Don Quixote, my Sancho Panza (Kyri) is dozing in the next chair, helping to keep me (somewhat) balanced.

Truly, I am blessed.

I hope I get to stay in the area, and in a way that not only continues to fuel the unfolding realization of my dreams but brings me joy. However, that's not today's concern. Nor is it tomorrow's. In this moment, the star is reachable, the dream is possible and the quest is far from hopeless. Who could ask for anything more?

Day 65

Wednesday, July 31
Tustin / Santa Ana, California

DAWN

If each day is a new birth, metaphorically speaking, and if the original birth, way back when, was difficult, could that explain why first thing in the morning — first thing *awake* — has so often been challenging for me?

I have no idea what my physical birth was like; my mother never spoke of it. But as I lie in bed wondering why I felt fine the instant I opened my eyes, then almost immediately spiraled into terror, I have to ask the question.

It reminds me of a rebirthing session I experienced more than twenty years ago when I was living in Penetanguishene, a period I chronicle in *Dialogues with the Divine*. The session was wrenching and emotionally exhausting: Despite the therapist's gentle coaxing, I couldn't bring myself to "come out."

The surrogate womb was warm, dark and felt safe. In there, I was invisible. And if I couldn't be seen, I couldn't be hurt. As a stand-in for the original, this womb felt nourishing and nurturing. All my needs were met. Nothing was demanded of me, other than to be.

Why leave when outside was, well...outside was the world, with all its hazards. Outside was the world, with all its demands. Outside was the world, with all its drama. Outside was the world, with all its struggles. It didn't feel safe out there. It had sure never been easy.

Who wouldn't prefer to stay cocooned in safety? And who, as an adult with that emotional history, wouldn't want to remain in the most womb-like place we have access to? That's right: in bed, tucked in under the covers, secure in the darkness...where nothing and no one can get at us.

I never made the direct connection between mornings and the womb before now. Yet it feels right, at least for me. And it ties in with some of the personal issues I have touched on through these chronicles, issues that are more relevant than ever as I am pushed out of hiding to walk the earth clothed only in my truth, more nakedly than ever. It's especially true on this journey, when each new waking day seems to be littered with more hazards to my perceived safety and security than the one before.

Having made the connection, I wish I could say I feel freer and lighter, ready to leap out of bed and eager to face the world. I don't. I'm still under the covers as I write this on my phone. But in this deeper understanding of why I experience most mornings as I do, I would like to think that I will soon be able to open my eyes to the new day with excitement and anticipation instead of fear and dread.

As for this day, I have decisions to make, some of which have already triggered my anxiety. Not one of them, however, must be made in this moment. In this moment, I am being greeted by the unconditional love of my dog, and it is to his needs I must attend. As such, it's time to get up and out for our walk, a walk that generally helps me move into my day with more hope and optimism, regardless of where I am or how I woke up.

MORNING

Now that dog and dad have been walked and breakfasted and I have revisited what I wrote earlier, I have some additional thoughts...

"All my needs of the moment were met. Nothing was demanded of me, other than to be." As I reread these two sentences, it strikes me that this is precisely how I am being called to live right now. It is how I have always been called to live, how most spiritual traditions call on all of us to live: in the moment and from the heart.

The absolute, fundamental truth is that if we live from the heart, the world outside the womb is no more dangerous than the world inside it. When we live from that moment-to-moment place, all our needs *are* met and nothing is demanded of us.

In this moment, I have my health, food for me and Kyri, a roof over my head and gas in the car (whose monthly payment isn't due for another eight days). In this moment, I am writing, which lies at the core of my heart's desire, and nothing is being demanded of me other than to be in this moment and to be present on this journey, wherever it takes me and however it gets me there.

In truth, *this* moment is as womb-like as it gets.

When I left Portland sixty-five days ago, I doubted I had the financial resources to keep going for more than two weeks. But like the story of Hanukkah, where one night's oil somehow kept the light burning for eight days, I continue to be fueled by timely miracles.

Even as the work that has long supported me has mostly dried up and new opportunities have yet to emerge, I somehow continue to attract the resources I need, often in the most unpredictable and random-seeming ways. The challenge, of course, is to stay in that womb-like place of knowing that just as my needs have always been met and are being met today, they will always be met.

The "how" is neither my concern nor my job. The "staying in the place of knowingness" is.

If I'm not perfect at it, I'm doing my best. Penning these chronicles helps enormously. All writing does.

Starbucks, Newport Coast, CA
Late Afternoon

I have written as vulnerably as this before, in *Dialogues with the Divine* and *Acts of Surrender*, but I have never "published" immediately in a forum that supports instant feedback; i.e., Facebook. As scary as it feels some days, I know it's the right thing to do, not least because it's important for me to get past those comments that, however loving their motivation, trigger my too-easily surfaced doubts, fears and insecurities.

I don't know what I'm going to do tomorrow, although I know what my fear would have me do. For this moment, for this breath, as fearless as I *don't* feel in many moments, I trust that I'm on the right path and in the right place: working on my *Bard of Bryn Doon* screenplay a block from the ocean at one of my favorite cafes in the country, with my canine companion at my side.

Somehow, today has taken care of me. I have to trust that tomorrow will do likewise. No, I have to do more than trust. I have to know.

August 2019

It's never too late to follow your dreams.
Sara's Year

No fear is stronger than you are. No fear is more powerful than you are. No fear can stand in your way, unless you choose to allow it that freedom.
The Book of Messages: Writings Inspired by Melchizedek

Day 66

Thursday, August 1
TUSTIN / SANTA ANA, CALIFORNIA

EARLY AFTERNOON

"I've been holding myself back," a friend confessed to me yesterday evening, and as soon as she did I saw this Fool's Journey I'm on through a radically new lens.

The Fool archetype holds, but another, deeper imperative is now at play as well: Through this journey, I am busting through all the ways I have held myself back, all the ways I have played small, all the ways I have stayed hidden, all the ways I have let myself succeed only to the extent that I felt safely cocooned from serious criticism and judgment.

I have already written about this to some extent. Yet those five words — "I've been holding myself back" — collected all my disparate thoughts on the subject into a single, concisely descriptive container, one that encapsulates what feels like a lifetime theme. And although I have chipped away at the walls keeping me in my safety zone over the past thirty-plus years, through my books, talks, workshops, coaching and related activities, I have done it in micro-bits, unconsciously keeping my readers, clients and audiences small enough that I was unlikely to attract much blowback (or praise, for that matter).

Better to "live small" while pretending to "live large" than to risk annihilation (my child-self's fear) by no longer holding myself back...by letting go into my version of the greatness that is everyone's birthright.

There's no judgment, regret or recrimination. I have always done my best to act from the highest place I can access in any given moment based on what I know in my heart to be true. Consequently, everything that has led up to this moment is in perfection, as is this moment.

At the same time, to be suddenly conscious of a lifelong pattern is to be given an opportunity to transform that restrictive pattern into one that's more expansive.

These writings and the act of posting them publicly while they're still fresh and I'm still raw is part of that chipping-away. Not being (overly) triggered by the comments and messages they elicit is another part. A big part.

What does that mean in practical terms? I'm not certain, other than that the clarity feels like a major breakthrough.

This afternoon, sitting at a shaded picnic table in an Orange County park on the first day of a new month in the shadow of a new moon, all I know is to "stay the course," at least for today.

As for tomorrow, it will reveal itself when it needs to and play out as it needs to.

For now, I'll take Kyri for a stroll and, unless a more pressing imperative shows up, "stay the course" by going to Starbucks to work on my screenplay.

Starbucks, Newport Coast, California
Afternoon

I'm not working on my screenplay. I can't stop thinking about those five words — *I've been holding myself back* — and about the breakthrough in awareness they represent. Is that why I came to Southern California? Why I keep returning to Southern California?

Now that I have the breakthrough in awareness, what do I do with it? How do I translate awareness into action? Where do I take that action?

Although Southern California is where I would choose for that breakthrough to play out, I might not be in a position to act on that choice. Many revolutionary inner shifts and at least as many extraordinary miracles got me here. But I can't see how they will keep me here beyond today. I have pushed myself so far over the edge on this journey that I'm not sure whether I can grapple my way back onto the ledge. And while I have called up more faith, courage and trust than I ever thought I possessed to carry me this far, the superhuman amounts needed to stick around may be more than I can access and express.

What does my heart say? I've spent a lot of time over these past sixty-six days listening for that voice and to that voice. I need to reach out to it again, now, because, truly, I don't know what to do.

I keep feeling the need to stay in Southern California, but how, without ending up on the street? A friend has suggested I hole up somewhere *not* in Southern California to regroup. That would be giving up...a kind of hiding, which in light of recent realizations is precisely what I'm trying to *not* do.

The one option that makes sense to me right now is to leave the hotel in the morning and drive north, I guess. Again. Back toward Oregon, I guess. Again.

I don't know. What do I do?

Be still. Be still and be in the heart of yourself, the heart of your journey, the heart of your path. Be still and know that you will never be abandoned, have never been abandoned, could never be abandoned.

You reflect on others' words and wonder if you are on the wrong track. You are not. Others' paths, outlooks and spiritual world views are theirs. Yours are yours. The gift here, as it has been before, is to reaffirm your path, outlook and spiritual world view. Hold fast and firm to what you know in your heart to be true. Don't let others' fears becomes yours.

I feel alone and lonely.

You walk a solitary path and are learning a level of self-reliance that you have never before needed to access. Of course, you feel alone and lonely. It's lonely at the top.

The top!!!??!? I'm so close to the bottom that I'm practically crawling on my belly.

In your perceived physical and material circumstances, perhaps. Not in your vibration.

If the vibration is destroying my physical and material circumstances, if the vibration, through my words and work, is reaching only the tiniest handful of people, most of whom don't get it, what good does it do me? For that matter, what's the point of this dialogue if I can't afford to eat or find a place to sleep.

You will not be homeless. You will not need to live in your car.

You say that, yet I am clearly running out of financial resources... and apparent options. Tomorrow morning, I must leave the area (to do what?) or somehow (how?) stay. I know it's not possible to run out of miracles, but it feels as though I have.

You have not because you cannot.

I want to stay, but I'm terrified that I'm being set up to be stranded. How much closer to the edge do you intend to push me?

As close to the edge as it takes.

To...?

Trust.

Haven't I gone above and beyond on that score?

You have done well.

But...?

This is not about measuring and measurements. This is about movement. This is about the dream, the life of your deepest dreams.

If something major or even medium-major doesn't move soon, it will become the life of my darkest nightmares.

You will not be abandoned.

I wonder if our definitions of abandonment are the same...

You will not run out of money. You will not lose any more credit.

You will not be homeless. You will not have to sleep in your car. You will not lose your car. Is that clear enough?

Yes, if you're not messing with me.

And you will not have to leave Southern California tomorrow.

Those are big promises.

You have big dreams.

Tustin / Santa Ana, CA
EVENING

Not for the first time this week, I spent too much of my day thinking about leaving California and trying to figure out where I would go. Back to Oregon? Back to Albuquerque? Back to Canada?

Also not for the first time this week, each time I settled down enough to meditate, the only thing that felt right, as insane as it sounds to me, was to stay put, at least for one more night…even if it means switching hotels. Any other choice would be holding myself back.

So that's the plan. It sounds irresponsible and possibly delusional, yet having come this far on this journey, I don't see how I can turn back.

In a phone conversation before I initiated this afternoon's inner dialogue, a friend and I ran through options of places I might go to from here. When we were done, I told her that none of them felt right.

"Given what you're experiencing there right now, does where you are feel right?" she asked.

"It's the only place that does," I sighed.

It's hard to go with what you know to be right when the perceived risk of failure is obscenely high, when that failure feels disturbingly imminent, when friends online and off think you are at best wrong or at worst certifiable, and when saying yes feels like the scariest and craziest thing you've ever done.

But if I say no, I will never know what might have been. I will always wonder what amazing things might have happened had I stayed.

All I can do, now as every day, is take it moment-by-moment, do the best I can in each of those moments and make the highest choice I can in each of those moments.

There's a good chance I'll wake up tomorrow shouting "no way in hell." That's why I'm writing this now: so I can read it again and again and again in the morning should I plunge back into terror and second-guessing.

Who knows? Maybe, for the first time, I will be fine in my knowingness and not need the reassurance of these words. Yet even if it's not true tomorrow, it will be true one of these days. In a world of increasing uncertainty, that's one thing I wish I wasn't certain of.

Day 67

Friday, August 2
Tustin / Santa Ana, California

EARLY MORNING

I'm nearly at the moment of choice. Stay or go. Check out or extend my stay. I have to decide by eleven.

Here's the good news: Enough donations came in overnight to buy me another night here. But...do I blow the whole amount on a single night? Do I ration the money out to last more nights by looking for somewhere cheaper? Do I use it to start getting me the hell out of California?

My wisest self is asking what I want. I want to be able to stay where I am, through the weekend...or longer. That, however, would require another miracle.

Without that new miracle, spending every dollar of these recent donations for only one additional night feels wise (I meant to type *un*wise) and irresponsible.

Is it wise? Was that Freudian slip the true answer? How wise would it be to let a typo determine my fate? I need to ponder that for a bit.

MORNING

I hoped I might have more clarity and feel better after breakfast. I don't. If it's possible, I feel worse.

In fact, unless these words somehow inspire me to keep going or some new miracle — a *big* miracle — shows up, I think I'm done.

Whatever that means in practical terms, I don't think I can keep going.

I know I have felt that before and come around before. Maybe I will this time, too. From where I sit, though, two hours before I have to either be out of this hotel room or have dropped every dime that came in last night to stay until tomorrow, I'm beyond done. I can't go on living like this. I don't *want* to go on living like this. I'm not sure I want to go on living, if it's going to be like this for much longer.

You (if there is a you) will say "look how far you've come" or "how can you look back on your life and question this?" or "don't give up on the dream." I feel like Yhoshi in that *MoonQuest* scene where he calls bullshit on the quest they're on. Fortunately for his companions, he ultimately comes around, with Toshar to help him see the light, his light. Unfortunately for me, my inner Toshar isn't up to the task this morning.

Have I finally been pushed over the edge? Have I let the siren song of an impossible dream throw me against the rocks of homelessness and destitution? I keep being reassured that I won't be abandoned. If this is what non-abandonment looks like, it's not reassuring.

I'm not out of money. But at this rate, as things look "in this moment," it's imminent. And although I'm profoundly grateful for last night's donations, I have to wonder whether they're anything more than a bunch of fingers trying to plug a dam that is so battered that it's beyond help...and hope.

When I wrote earlier, it felt as though the highest use of the donations was on another night here. Now, I can't see how that's possible.

How can I have been so foolish as to believe this would work out in any way other than the disaster that it's shaping up to be? How could I have been so foolish as to trust enough to rent that Portland condo in the first place, only to have the whole experience go up in flames and send me here to...to what?

Maybe running away from Southern California is continuing to play small, continuing to hold myself back. But Jesus fucking

Christ, how much more do I have to trust? However much it is, I don't think I can do it.

I hope you have something to offer other than empty words here, O Wisest Self. Because if not, well, I don't know what I'll do.

For now, though, there's a decision I must make.

MID-MORNING

A few minutes ago, I muscle-tested on the options, which are...

- extend my stay here by one night (or longer, although that doesn't appear to be financially possible);
- check out and book into somewhere cheap (or at least cheaper) in the broad general area, if such a thing exists; or
- get the hell out of Dodge and head for...?

Staying another night won out. Am I throwing my money away?

Be still. Be still and know the God That You Are, the being of infinite wisdom, grace and power that you are. No one but a being of such power would be able to move through what you are moving through.

I think of Jesus crying, "My God, why hast thou forsaken me?" And I think of the painful end he came to. Yes, there was resurrection...but at what an awful cost.

The cost of his limited humanness?

Not reassuring. In that case, take me now and get the whole damn thing over with.

Be still, beloved. Be still and know how loved you are, how protected you are, how in constant grace you are. What else but grace could explain how nearly the precise amount, almost to the penny, showed up in time to let you stay where you are one more night?

And then?

Let "and then" take care of itself.

What if you were to extend your stay by another night, then get on with your day?

What if you were to return to Newport Coast, that place of infinite possibility you feel it to be, and just be in that place, letting infinite possibility unfold and manifest into your life?

What if you were to write about this experience, or write on your screenplay or simply take in the beauty and grace of that place, the perfect mirror of your beauty and grace?

What if you were to allow yourself to live another day in the place that brings you such joy and let tomorrow take care of itself? What if...?

If only *you* could experience the stress and anxiety that each day brings.

How much of your stress is strictly about money and finances, and how much is about being in Southern California and in this vibration of no-hiding? Ask yourself. Now.

I'm asking...

Between seventy-five and eighty percent of my anxiety is unrelated to money and finances. It's hard to believe. But most of my stress appears to be related to being here, to coming out of hiding, to being fully me in the world. Even the remaining twenty to twenty-five percent isn't entirely about money.

Does that not tell you how strong you have grown? You are not scared of running out of money, not primarily. In a sense, you are scared of the opposite, of having more money than you know what to do with. You are scared of who you are becoming. Can you let yourself be what you are becoming? Can you?

I don't know...

Here's what I do know: I'll extend my stay here by another night. I'll drive back to yesterday's hiking trail for lunch, then down to the coast. It all feels beyond futile, but I will give it one more night. One...unless something shifts by morning.

Go, then. And let the story unfold as it unfolds.

Starbucks, Newport Coast, CA
Late Afternoon

A roller coaster, miracle-filled day...

1. Money came in (hallelujah!), if only enough to keep me in place another night. *Stay in the moment, Mark David.*
2. Emotions were all over the map, from unconditional trust to "I can't do this anymore" and back again. *Be gentle with yourself, Mark David.*
3. Online feedback to my journey today has ranged from loving support ("keep it up") to confusion ("I don't get what you're doing") to disdain ("your donations are taking money from those who really need it"). *Hold your center, Mark David.*
4. The folks who finance my car agreed to defer this month's payment. *See, Mark David? Another miracle.*
5. After stressing over whether to stay in my hotel another night, move somewhere cheaper that's considerably farther away or get the hell out of California, I extended my stay by a single night, only to discover that the rate for tonight is considerably lower than the one I was quoted yesterday. *See, Mark David? Wasn't all that worry a lot of pointless drama?*
6. I had a random conversation with a woman here at Starbucks this afternoon about writing and coaching. And although she didn't buy any of my books or sign up for a coaching session on the spot, she did take information from me on my *Organic Screenwriting* book. *See, Mark David? Energy is moving.*
7. I'm doing what I can to stay in the place of miracle and infinite possibility, the only place to be when faced with the logically impossible and conventionally improbable. *You're doing great!*

When I lived on Maui eighteen years ago, my sound-healing practice and multiple concurrent jobs barely brought in enough to keep us (me, my then-wife and our young daughter) above water (no pun intended). We couldn't afford to stay on the island, and we couldn't afford to leave.

When we decided to move there from the Big Island, our hope had been to live in the upcountry Kula hills, but it proved too expensive. Instead, we lived among the tourists in less-pricey Kihei.

A few times a month, we would drive up to Kula to connect with the energy of the place. Up there, with the struggle of life in Kihei miles away and hundreds of feet below, anything seemed possible. Renewed and recharged, we would drive back down the mountain to face "real life."

We never did get to live in Kula, but miracle and infinite possibility showed up another way: A wealthy sound-healing client of mine fronted us the money to return to the mainland.

I thought a lot about our Kula experiences this morning when I felt guided to return to this Starbucks-by-the-sea that has been my haunt for as long as I have been staying a reasonable drive away.

Why? Well, after I left Starbucks yesterday afternoon, I walked Kyri around Crystal Cove Shopping Center, stopping at a bench overlooking the ocean. As I watched the sun lowering itself toward the sea, it struck me that this, like Kula, feels like a place of infinite possibility. Whenever I'm here, I sense no blocks or barriers in my life, only flow. No wonder I keep being pulled back, and no wonder it has been such a place of creative flow for me over the years.

So, in the midst of this morning's anxiety when it felt once again important to spend the afternoon here, I thought back to Kula and understood why, even if it made no logical sense.

I still don't know what I'll do tomorrow. Hopefully, I learned enough from today's freak-out to not melt down about it in the morning. But staying in the area feels like the absolute right strategy, however on the edge it keeps me. And as I sit here on this Starbucks patio toward the end of another summer afternoon, I'm certain that anything, absolutely anything, is possible.

May it be so.

Tustin / Santa Ana, California
EVENING

As I was driving back to the hotel this evening (I almost wrote "home," though if Johnny Mercer was right when he wrote "Any Place I Hang My Hat Is Home," I *was* driving home), I reflected on the five months I spent in rural Ontario two decades ago.

Among the many reasons I thought I was up there was to work on a draft of *The MoonQuest*. And while I did some work on the manuscript, I ended up spending most of my time writing a book I hadn't planned to write and didn't initially realize I was writing.

Dialogues with the Divine: Encounters with My Wisest of Self began as a private chronicle of the emotional healing I was experiencing at the time and consisted of a series of inner dialogues, much like the ones I shared yesterday and earlier today. It would be fifteen years before more than a handful of people got a chance to read it.

What brought all that to mind? When I left Portland, I was hoping to use any available writing time during my travels to work on my new *Q'ntana* story. Instead, as happened back in Penetanguishene all those years ago, I have found myself immersed in an altogether different series of writings — these writings.

My *Dialogues with the Divine* manuscript found its natural conclusion when I left my rural Ontario hideaway and returned, unexpectedly, to Toronto. What (not to mention where and when) will these writings' natural conclusion be? It's hard to imagine a parallel return to Portland. But who knows...

Day 68

Saturday, August 3
STARBUCKS, NEWPORT COAST, CALIFORNIA

AFTERNOON

I'm back at my Starbucks, sipping an Americano while trying to catch my breath from the astounding events of the past couple of hours. This afternoon, in another astonishing piece of synchronicity, I got to visit with Brendalyn Batchelor, a Unity minister friend from New Mexico who happens to be in Southern California this week and is staying a ten-minute drive from my hotel.

We met over cold drinks and cookies at the home of her friend Marj Britt, retired senior minister of Unity of Tustin. Brendalyn has followed some of my Facebook posts, but Marj knew nothing about me or this journey. So I recounted my story from the beginning, going beyond the superficial facts to share my take on the emotional and spiritual essence of it.

About an hour into our time together, Marj emerged from the kitchen with what I can only describe as a "visionary insight." Perhaps my true mission at this time, she enthused, is to live among the homeless as the spiritual master I am and help them tell their stories. She even offered me a contact; she described him as an "angel on a motorcycle," someone who is already living and working with the homeless.

A few hours later, after lunch and a tour of the Unity of Tustin campus, I thanked Marj, hugged her and Brendalyn goodbye, got back into the car and crashed — emotionally.

One of my biggest fears since my Portland life began to

disintegrate was that I would end up homeless. And here was a spiritual master suggesting I choose it as my highest path. I was devastated...and confused.

I'm still confused.

Tustin / Santa Ana, California
EVENING

I woke up this morning aware that two months from today I turn sixty-five and, amazingly, given the radical uncertainty of my life and considerably more radical on-the-edgeness of my living situation, I didn't freak out. To my surprise, in fact, I was pretty cool with it all.

Four things probably helped: some fresh financial miracles, two songs in my head as I woke up and a Facebook reminder about a meme I posted a few years ago on this day.

The first song was the ultimate anthem of self-confidence and bald chutzpah, *Funny Girl*'s "Don't Rain on My Parade," which warns all comers against getting in the way of Fanny Brice's dream. Who could feel hopeless after that?

The second was a Hebrew prayer, "Mi Chamocha," which is a sort of Jewish equivalent of the Christian hymn "How Great Thou Art." Hearing "Mi Chamocha" reminded me of a newsletter piece I wrote some fifteen years ago. In it I insisted that the God of "How Great Thou Art" was not some external, white-whiskered guy on a heavenly throne or anything at all external to us, but an essential, integral part of each of us.

"How great is the God in each of us," I wrote. "How great is the indwelling spirit that resides within every one of us. How great is our wisest self. From that place of infinite wisdom, how great *we* are."

It's hard not to feel upbeat after a reminder like that.

Finally, on this day in 2015 I posted a meme featuring a quote from actor Patricia Routledge (Hyacinth Bucket in TV's *Keeping Up Appearances*): "Once you're willing to risk everything, you can accomplish anything."

I have taken many risks in my life, though none as huge as the one I'm taking now. If I am not risking absolutely everything, I have come pretty damn close. Perhaps I can, then, accomplish anything.

After I reposted the Routledge quote, I posted another meme, a quote from *The MoonQuest*: "Once you let yourself dream the impossible, the impossible will come to pass."

How can I write words like that and not live them? I've asked myself that question a lot over the past nearly ten weeks, each time I have been tempted to give up, which is more often than I care to admit.

How can I not follow the voice of my heart when everything I have taught and written over the past three decades is a call for others to follow theirs — in their lives as much as in their writing?

Those were some of the questions I asked myself after hearing Marj's "vision." She had proposed a noble calling for me. Was it mine? It didn't feel like it. Maybe I was in denial. Or maybe I hadn't been ready to hear it until today. Could she be wrong? Or was she right and that's why I have felt so pulled to Southern California?

A few hours later, when I got to my "place of infinite possibilities" — the Starbucks at Newport Coast — I initiated one of my meditative inner-dialogue journaling sessions, hoping it would help take me deeper than my surface anxiety.

I didn't want to eliminate the possibility that Marj had tapped into something I hadn't been ready to hear until that moment. Yet I couldn't ignore the fact that what she shared conflicted with my sense of my own knowingness.

What follows is an abridged version of that conversation…

Is it in my highest good to take Marj's intuitive hit literally? Could my next spiritual call be to live among the homeless (i.e., to be homeless by choice, in a tent in a homeless encampment) as some sort of "spiritual master in disguise," as Marj put it, to help them tell their stories?

Would that be such a bad life? Would it be an unfulfilling life?

Is that a yes?

It is neither a yes nor a no. It is simply a question.

It's a question, although there's nothing "simply" about it. Yes, it could be a high calling. Everyone deserves to tell their stories; no one more, perhaps, than the dispossessed. Given that we're answering questions with questions, I have another one for you: I'll admit it could be a good idea; but to quote all my books for writers, is it the *right* idea for me for right now?

What do you think?

It's hard to get past what I think to what I know.

You are reluctant to dismiss it out of hand because of who and what Marj Britt is?

That's part of it.

Do you consider yourself to be as wise and enlightened a spiritual teacher and guide as Marj Britt is? Leave your ego mind out of the answer, both the self-aggrandizing part and the self-esteem-challenged part. What does your heart say? What does your heart know?

My heart says yes. At the same time, I don't want to be too proud to be open to others' intuitive suggestions. And Marj Britt is, well—

A master? What did Mary Omwake[1] call you?

A master.

What does the master in you say?

That Marj's comment was designed to trigger me in precisely the way it did, though probably not intentionally. It tempted me to defer to someone else's wisdom, the wisdom of a *perceived* spiritual superior, instead of relying on my own. It triggered my fears that my inner guidance was flawed.

And...?

---

1. After attending one of my classes at Unity of Maui where she was then the senior minister and I was a congregant, Mary Omwake announced, "Mark David Gerson is a master, one of the great teachers."

Given my easily ignited financial anxieties, it caused me to question whether I can ever get out of what seems a downward spiral and avoid being forced onto the street.

And...?

The good news is I'm less willing to defer to Marj. The bad news is that the financial anxiety hasn't gone away. The good news is it's not as acute as it was.

Do you believe in the dream?

It's hard not to wonder whether I'm being pushed onto the street regardless of what my heart is saying.

Can you believe that you will not be homeless, at least no more homeless than you are today? Can you believe that you will not be forced to downgrade your accommodations? Can you believe that you are home? Can you know it? All of it?

I have to breathe into those. Yes. One hundred percent.

Then Marj Britt did what she needed to do for you. She was an instrument of Spirit, even if it was not the instrument she thought she was being. So bless her and be grateful, as you bless and be grateful to all those who challenge you, disagree with you, judge you and criticize you. They are your teachers. They are propelling you forward into your calling, into the dream.

Write and share your stories. That is your primary calling and dream...your primary mission and responsibility. Clear away all inner barriers to their widest promulgation. Find your voice. Free your words into the world with more force and fearlessness than ever before, and let them effect the transformation that is their calling.

I felt better after that. Who wouldn't? But as my mind wandered out of the moment and on to tomorrow and the days after, wondering how any of that could be possible given what felt to be the insanely precarious state of my finances, my fear took over again...which is when I began writing this.

That was an hour ago. Now, severe cramps (fear) and many words later, I have regained some semblance of equilibrium (writing nearly always helps). What will I do tomorrow, let alone in the next days? No idea, and when I tried to meditate on it, I got not to ask until the morning.

I have made a provisional commitment to stick around at least one more day by booking Kyri for a vet appointment in Yorba Linda tomorrow afternoon for his shots. Beyond that, my mind goes into overwhelm. So, the rest of tomorrow's answers will have to wait until tomorrow.

Day 69

Sunday, August 4
Tustin / Santa Ana, California

MORNING

Is today the day I give up? Is today the day I say I can't do this anymore and mean it? And stick to it?

I got through yesterday, the day that was two months shy of my sixty-fifth birthday, the day that a retired Unity minister suggested I choose homelessness as part of my spiritual work, the day that marked nearly ten weeks on this journey-beyond-folly, the day that no dramatic miracle showed up to offer me enough hope to continue.

It's 6:35 in the morning. I've been awake for a couple of hours, trying to get back to sleep. Instead, I feel sick to my stomach.

Yes, I could stay here another night. As it has for nearly the week I have been here, my inner guidance urges me to do just that. But why? I'm not sure what the point would be or how many more days I could sustain this. Three? Not if I choose to continue to eat. Not if I continue to pay those bills I am still paying. Not if I have my car's oil changed (a full thirty-thousand-mile servicing is out of the question for now).

Kyri will be okay. I've got plenty of food for him and his shots this afternoon can go on CareCredit, which I can't use for much else these days. As for me, I'm not sure anymore.

My Social Security hits my bank account in a week. Unfortunately, as things stand right now, I don't have a week. Besides, Social Security would be little more than a band-aid.

I should check out of the hotel today and....and do what? Sleep in the car?

Who knows? I'm too busy questioning nearly every decision I have ever made to get any clarity about what to do for today.

Have I run out of options? Do I even know what my options are anymore? Neither staying nor leaving makes any sense...not that anything about this foolish journey ever did.

The best option for right now is to drag myself out of bed, walk Kyri, see if I can settle my stomach enough to keep some breakfast down, then make some sort of decision. About the day, certainly. About my life moving forward, perhaps.

I can't go on like this.

Starbucks, Newport Coast, California
Late Afternoon

If I'm not in as bad a way as I was eleven hours ago, I'm not doing great. Being here in Newport Coast helps. Sort of. Today, this place feels more inaccessible than ever. And the Porsche 911 that parked in front of me when I got here felt more mocking than inspiring.

Earlier this afternoon, I was on the phone with a friend most of the way down from Yorba Linda, where Kyri got his shots, and I was more and more angry and inconsolable, not least because every suggestion he made only reinforced the futility of this journey and panicked me more. At least he gets it, which is more than most people do. Other friends are sympathetic and try to be supportive, yet it often feels as though they are responding from their fear, which although understandable, isn't helpful when I'm terrified.

What now? Another day is nearly done, and I don't know what the fuck to do, about anything. I'm angry and scared. Plus, I feel abandoned and betrayed. And don't throw the "you either trust" quote[2] at me. I'm not in the mood. And don't tell me to "be still and

---

2. "You either trust or you do not. There's no halfway in between." This quote shows up in all my *Legend of Q'ntana* books — at least as much for the author as for readers.

know I'm loved." Who/whatever you are, you have a twisted way of showing it.

Apart from my "detour" out of Kingman a few weeks ago, I can't think of a single instance where I haven't listened to and heeded the voice of my heart. And this is what it has come to?

I'm trapped. I can't afford to stay, and I can't afford to leave, like on Maui. I never felt good about asking for financial help to get off the island back then. I guess I've gotten over that.

> *You are scared and angry, and you feel betrayed and abandoned. You feel as though you have been pushed off a cliff and the loving arms of God are no longer there to catch you[3]. You look at your day-to-day situation and predict nothing but disaster. You wonder whether it's wise to be dismissing friends' suggestions, Marj's vision and others' criticism. You second-guess the voice of your heart because you see it to be leading you into mortal danger. You are reluctant to have this conversation because you doubt its long-term value, even if it makes you feel better for a few hours. You doubt the utility of having come to Newport Coast for similar reasons. Have we missed anything?*

The swear words. And the intense emotion behind everything you said.

> *Know this, again: You have neither been betrayed nor abandoned.*

Spiritually, no one is ever abandoned, regardless of their fate. I get that, and it's terrific from a higher perspective. I don't find it reassuring down here.

Am I being stripped of absolutely everything, until all I have left is radical homelessness? If so, I suppose that's flattering, in that

---

3. In a nightmare many years ago, I'm clinging to the roof-ledge of an early skyscraper, my feet dangling high above the pavement. "Let go," a voice repeats gently but insistently. I peer down at the street far below and grip more tightly. I can't do it. Twice over the next days, I take that scene into meditation. Each time, I try to let go; each time, I can't. Finally, on a third try, I do...not because I'm braver, but because the pain of holding on has become unbearable. To my surprise, instead of hurtling to the pavement, I float feather-like into what I can only describe as "the arms of God."

navigating a situation like this takes a high level of mastery. Well, I don't have that kind of mastery.

Has everything I have been guided to believe by "the voice of my heart" been one ruse after another?

I almost feel like I felt on July 17 when I turned north out of Kingman instead of continuing west toward California: with no foundation, no rudder and little belief. I feel as though not only this place and that Porsche in the parking lot are mocking me, but as though all the books I have written are also mocking me…as though so much of the past thirty-something years has been a colossal waste of energy and effort.

You don't seriously believe any of that, do you?

Most of it? No. But it's true that I'm hard-pressed to know what to believe and trust anymore…to know what is *truly* in my highest good to do and be.

What do you want?

I want to be able to stay in Southern California in a way that doesn't force me to move limited funds from my hemorrhaging bank account to a different credit card every two days…that doesn't strip me of my remaining resources…that doesn't force me to live out of my car, in a tent among the homeless or on the street.

I want to live, not merely survive. I want to do more than live; I want to thrive.

I want to live the life of my dreams, not the life of my nightmares.

I want my words to transform the consciousness of millions.

I want to feel as though my life is building toward something, not disintegrating into nothing.

Can you believe that all you are experiencing is moving you in that direction?

Not anymore. Where's the evidence? Nor do I see how I can continue to stay the course — practically or emotionally. Like I said earlier: I can't go on like this, but I don't know what else to do. I'm not sure I know how to trust anymore.

If nothing substantive has changed by morning, I'll check out and start driving — north toward Oregon or east toward Albuquerque. And I'll probably start sleeping in the car. Because, honestly, I don't know what else to do.

If you can't trust in this moment, that's okay. You have lost your faith before, and it has always returned. Let it all go for now. Your faith will be waiting for you when you are again ready for it.

I'm not convinced, but Kyri needs walking and I need food for dinner. It's time to move on.

Tustin / Santa Ana, CA
EVENING

Is every day's "report from the field" the same? At some point, generally first thing in the morning, I say something like, "I can't do this anymore"; at some other point, often when I am in Newport Coast near the water, I relax (somewhat) back into the journey.

The major difference from one day to the next is the scale, intensity and frequency of my anxiety attacks, doubts and second-guessing.

Today was much the same. And once again, as I walk Kyri in the gathering dusk that marks the end of another mini-journey on this larger one, my heart and my fears have different agendas for tomorrow.

Even as my heart remain steadfast in its urgings, the fearful parts of me are locked in doubt...when they are not recoiling in panic. From their perspective, it has grown nearly impossible (if not already impossible) to stay in Southern California and equally impossible to leave.

A half-dozen steps after I dictated that sentence into my phone, I passed and photographed the "flight" sign that's a landmark feature of the Flight at Tustin Legacy development. That word captures the dichotomy and duality I often struggle with: The word can either represent soaring freely through the heavens or fleeing in panic.

My fear would have me flee. My heart would have me soar. My fear points to the increasingly alarming state of my finances. My heart points to the miracles that have, incredibly, kept this journey going far longer than seemed possible at the outset. Yes, there have been casualties; my credit score, for example. But the gifts, inner and outer, far outweigh anything as superficial as a credit score, however valuable that little number can be in daily life.

What will I do tomorrow? My fear shrieks, "Get the hell out of here." It doesn't matter that it can produce no viable suggestions about where to go and what to do when I get there. My heart whispers, "You are home, and you must hold on to the knowingness that miracles will continue to sustain you."

My fear offers mounting evidence of its position. Compelling evidence. My heart offers one word, "trust," along with decades of convincing results. Compelling results.

What will I do tomorrow? I'd like to say that I will continue to follow my heart. With each passing day, however, that becomes more and more challenging.

What will I do tomorrow? I don't know. I'm not even sure what I'll be in a position to do. So for now, all I can do is let it go as best I can and, somehow, trust that tomorrow will produce the necessary miracles to get me through another day, whatever the day's call turns out to be.

A final note...

Remember the Gateway Arch in St. Louis? Well, for the past week I have been staying across the road from a different arch, passing under it nearly every evening when I walk Kyri, not recognizing until tonight that, as a symbolic gateway into Tustin, it is a portal in its own right.

I'm not sure what that means for me, but it has to be significant. Now that I have made that connection, perhaps it will factor into whatever decision(s) I make in the morning.

That's tomorrow's business. For now, it's time for tea and cookies and a Kyri cuddle.

LATE EVENING

I'm ready to start my life here.

I haven't said that before. Until now, all I wanted was the peace of mind to know that I could stay in this hotel for more than one night at a time. But a bit ago, that sentence popped into my mind: "I'm ready to start my life here."

I'm ready to stay on in this hotel if that serves as a useful transition. I am also ready to begin the process of *living* here.

It's odd. I thought I was ready before now. But perhaps I was so caught up in the drama of lack that I wasn't able to make the leap from "being here" to "being ready to live here."

Maybe the difference sounds subtle. To *me*, it's huge. Maybe that's part of what that Tustin "portal" is all about.

Of course, I'm no more in a position to act on that readiness than I was before that sentence dropped into my awareness. Financially, I mean. But maybe — hopefully — my statement of readiness, my *feeling* of readiness, will finally shift the energy that will make it possible for me to do more than be here, but to *live* here.

May it be so. And soon.

Day 70

Monday, August 5
TUSTIN / SANTA ANA, CALIFORNIA

MORNING

It took me a couple of days to feel confident and secure enough to reach back out to Marj Britt. This is what I wrote this morning...

Dear Marj,

First, apologies for not having gotten back to you yesterday. As with most days these days, I had a lot of processing to do, with a little extra kicking in after our time together on Saturday.

Before anything else, I want to thank you for your hospitality and your insight. This can be a lonely journey sometimes, and connecting (or reconnecting in the case of Brendalyn) with like-spirited beings is always a wonderful and welcome gift.

As I knew you would expect me to do, I did my meditative due diligence on how or whether to act on the vision you received for me on Saturday. I owed it to you; more than that, I owed it to myself.

Without taking you through all I explored and all the inner guidance I received, let me say that even though I don't feel that Spirit is moving me in the directions you suggested, at least not at this time, you were definitely an instrument of Spirit.

Part of this journey for me has been to stay centered and grounded in my own guidance and to stand firmly (but not inflexibly) in what I know in my heart to be true for me in any given moment.

It has never been easy for me to stand in the presence of a spiritual master and teacher and not defer to his wisdom or her vision over my own. Yet that is one of the gifts you gave me on Saturday. It reminded me that I, too, am a spiritual master and teacher and that while I must remain open and flexible to others' insights, I must always run them through the filter of my own wisdom and mastery.

When I did that with the noble vision you painted for me, my heart advised me that while it could be a "good idea," given the surface view of my circumstances, and a noble calling in any circumstances, it was not the "right idea" or calling for me at this time.

So, although your gift may not have been the one you thought you were giving me, it was nonetheless a wondrous, strengthening and empowering one. And I am profoundly grateful for all the ways in which it will help me move forward as I continue day-by-day and moment-by-moment on this journey.

Blessings,
Mark David

Starbucks, Newport Coast, California
Afternoon

"I'm ready to start my life here." I couldn't anticipate what those seven words would unleash when they popped into my head yesterday evening. One minute, I was a wanderer; the next, I had landed.

There remain infinite unknowns. Although those seven words triggered an off-the-scale inner earthquake (the aftershocks are ongoing), the facts on the ground have yet to catch up. A few minor if significant miracles this morning bought me another night where I'm staying. But the earthshaking mega-miracle (or its first rumbling installment) that I hoped to wake to wasn't visible to me when I opened my eyes to this final day of my tenth week of journeying.

I spent most of the morning so overwhelmed that all I could do was take Kyri for a second walk (through the Tustin portal) and draft a thank-you note to Marj Britt.

If I had to experience overwhelm, I would have preferred for it to be by a pot of gold left at my door by some leprechaun. Instead, I felt the immensity of those seven words, even as I didn't know what to do with them.

Around noon, a friend texted me to see how I was doing. "It feels like I've come home," I dictated through Siri. When I felt those words pushing through me, I struggled to speak them aloud. When I could manage it, my voice caught with unexpected emotion.

On one level, of course, I have come home to myself. I'm more comfortable in my own skin and with my heart than I have ever been. That alone would be powerful and worth celebrating. But on this eighth consecutive day in Southern California, the longest I have stopped in the area — or anywhere — since leaving Portland, it's as though I have come home to a *place*. Finally.

I don't know the specifics of the place; this is a vast metropolitan area and I have spent time in only select bits of it. I certainly don't know the specifics of how. Both sets of details, apparently, are far above my human mind's pay grade. Both reside in the realm of the heart. Both, I must believe, are the responsibility of my wisest self.

I must do more than believe. I must *know*.

I must know, too, that if it's important for me to spend another day and night in this hotel, the means will make themselves available, as they did this morning for tonight.

Money wasn't today's only miracle. When I first inquired about staying on, I discovered that the hotel was sold out for tonight. Yet I somehow manifested not only a cancellation but a deep discount on tonight's standard rate, which is considerably higher than what I have been paying here thus far.

Tomorrow will take care of itself, as all tomorrows have for the past sixty-nine days, though I can't imagine how. How and where I will land more permanently in the area, if I'm meant to do so, will also have to take care of itself.

So what am I to do? Humans always wants to be *doing* something. When I go within to tap into inner guidance, I sense that wiser energies, heart energies, wisest-self energies, have the situation in hand. My human job, as always, is to keep my vibration up (i.e., stay out of fear) and keep writing — these chronicles, my screenplay and other in-progress and queued-up projects.

"Act as though and make it so," I write in *Acts of Surrender*. That, I was "told," is the third part of my job description: to move beyond readiness to start my life here and to act on that readiness. If I can't buy or rent anything yet (paying for accommodation one day at a time is all I can manage these days, barely), I can explore the area for communities that feel right. And if I can't yet update my car registration and driver's license (I would need a permanent address and a chunk of spare cash or credit for that), I can (as someone suggested to me this morning) replace "I'm on an open-ended road trip" with something like "I recently moved to the area," whenever the opportunity arises.

Bottom line? Whatever it means and however it plays out, I've come home.

Tustin / Santa Ana, California
LATE EVENING

If my mantra last night and this morning was "I'm ready to start my life here," tonight's, on the eve of the start of this journey's eleventh week, is "I am home, and I am making a life for myself here. Now. The life of my dreams."

It feels powerful and empowered to say it, yet it's hard to think of any place as home and have a good feeling about it when you can't stop yourself from wondering whether you will be forced to start sleeping in your car in a couple of days.

I do my best not to go there, and I have largely succeeded. Today, ironically, was one of the least stressful days I've experienced in what seems a long time...well, until a few hours ago.

Certainly, the whole notion of viewing my wandering as over and Southern California as home, which kicked in last night, felt strange today. Not stressed-out strange. More like incredulous strange. Good-incredulous strange.

Yet when I got back to the hotel a few hours ago and checked my finances, the old anxiety kicked in. It's that heart-truth versus mind-fear thing again. It's always that, isn't it? What we know in our hearts to be true versus our fear's limited view of what's possible.

What I need to keep remembering, even as my financials appear to portend disaster, is how I feel about being here — with my heart, not my head. What I need to keep remembering are the miracles that have carried me safely to this moment. What I need to keep remembering is the dream that quickens my heart and fires up my soul. What I need to keep remembering is who I am at my core; and who I am is my strength and my passion, not my fear.

All those can be difficult to remember when the voice of fear is so loud and the voice of the heart speaks only into the stillness.

So as I sit here in the gathering dusk of this sultry Tustin evening at the close of Day 70 and Week 10 of this journey, I try to quiet the shrieks of fear and listen for that small but mighty heart-voice, the one that reminds me of all I have achieved through this time and of all that I have received...that assures me that I am home, in this place as well in my heart...that sings of the magnificence that awaits me if I can hang on just a bit longer.

In this moment and not for the first time, I don't know how much longer I can hang on. I have been saying that nearly every day for the past few weeks, and each time I say it and however long I feel it, I always manage to hang on. Somehow.

I will tonight, too. Somehow. So I return to the mantra, which despite my anxiety, feels truer than my fear: "I am home, and I am making a life for myself here. Now. The life of my dreams."

I will speak the mantra again in a few minutes as I pass through the Tustin portal. I must do more than speak it. I must feel it. I must feel it in my heart, which is the source of all power, strength and truth. For it is only from that place that it can come to pass, in all its splendor and magnificence...and mine.

Day 71

Tuesday, August 6
TUSTIN / SANTA ANA, CALIFORNIA

EARLY MORNING

Has the dream finally imploded? It may well have. If I'm not totally tapped out, I'm close. Before I fell asleep last night, I said I needed a "substantial" miracle to keep me here. Instead, the reverse happened: A pending charge gobbled up the remaining credit on one of my surviving cards. (I have had to let a few cards go over the course of the summer.)

I might be able to get a few dollars trimmed off last night's hotel charge because my room wasn't cleaned yesterday, but that's nickel-and-dime stuff. The bottom line is that without a substantial influx of funds in the next hour or so, I'm out of here. Out of this hotel and out of the area. That is more than my fear talking; it's what I got in meditation.

MORNING

No influx of any sort, so I'm packing up to check out.

I don't know what to believe anymore, including when it comes to the inner guidance that has repeatedly insisted that I won't be homeless and forced to live out of my car. Right now, both are likely.

I'm considering heading back up to Mount Shasta, though not for spiritual reasons. Because I can more easily sleep in the car there. Beyond that...?

I'm done with all this. All of it. Frankly, if it weren't for my daughter and my dog, I might again consider driving off a cliff. What's the point in going on?

I'm done. So done.

Day 72

Wednesday, August 7
HAYWARD, CALIFORNIA

NOON

I did not expect to be back in Hayward today. But nor did I expect the emotional, spiritual and financial turbulence that began to seethe as I lay in bed Monday night, especially given how optimistic I'd felt only a few hours earlier. It broke into a furious boil when I woke up in a panic forty-five minutes later, then exploded through a sleepless night into Tuesday morning, when it became apparent just how completely my finances had collapsed.

Instead of the morning miracle I had hoped for, I got an anti-miracle: An unexpected overnight charge had wiped out my available credit. Not only could I not afford another night's stay where I was, I couldn't afford another night's stay anywhere.

Enter Ted and Rich, the Bay Area friends who have hosted me here twice before. Thanks to their generosity, I'm back with them for a couple of nights while I regroup. This wasn't the miracle I was expecting. Yet I have to concede that it's a miracle nonetheless.

It was impossible for me to view anything as miraculous during the first half of my drive up here yesterday. I spent it being angry, frightened, resentful and so on edge that I couldn't even talk to my closest friends. Even as random strands of fresh inner guidance tried to push through my resistance, I tuned them out. All my inner reserves of faith, trust and knowingness had evaporated. I felt depleted — spiritually as well as financially — and I swore I would never return to Southern California.

That's probably not true. I'm loath to admit it, but if called back I'll likely go. For now, I can't foresee an imminent return. Frankly, once I leave Hayward in the morning, it's hard to imagine how I'll make it through the rest of this week, anywhere.

My one hope is the possibility of a small copywriting job. A former client texted me about it this morning. Still, unless it comes through and he pays me in advance, I'm in no less of a bind.

As for tomorrow, maybe I'll aim for Sacramento. That's where my ex-client (soon to be my ex ex-client, I hope) is based. After that? Back to Mount Shasta, perhaps — less, as I noted yesterday, for its energy-activation/transformational potential and more because the ranger guardians of the Shasta-Trinity National Forest tolerate car-campers. And car-camping is free. My inner guidance continues to insist that I will never have to sleep in my car. In this moment, though, I'm not seeing any viable alternatives.

"In this moment." That's the key phrase in that last paragraph and the one I must keep repeating if I am to keep going. The question can no longer be "What am I to do today?" or "Where am I to go today?"; it has to be "What am I to do *in this moment?*"

In this moment, I will sign off from these jottings and consider working on my *Q'ntana* screenplay. The next moments, and days, will reveal themselves in their time, not mine. Somehow, I need to be okay with that.

Postscript: I dreamt last night that an ailing great aunt had changed her will to leave me her entire estate, worth a hundred thousand dollars. In reality, that great aunt died decades ago, and if she'd had a hundred grand, she sure didn't leave it to me. Perhaps the dream was telling me that an old part of me was nearing its time to die, and that its death would open the floodgates to more abundance.

Of course, nothing within us, any more than anything outside us, ever truly dies. It simply changes form. Whatever my great aunt represents is not being killed off; it's growing into a more evolved form of consciousness. Here's hoping that it's an evolved form of consciousness that can keep me afloat a while longer in this physical realm that is proving so problematic to me these days.

Hayward, CA
AFTERNOON

Something Ted asked me over lunch today prompted me to meditate on this question: "Is any part of me, even the teeniest, tiniest, smallest part, choosing struggle as part of my path to the desires of my heart and the life of my dreams?"

The answer I got surprised me. I fully expected a yes. Surely, some small part of me had made a conscious or unconscious choice to experience what sure feels like struggle. To be honest, I was hoping for a yes. That, at least, would give me something to work on, something that might shift things for the better.

Instead, I got an unambiguous no.

What you are experiencing is a form of alchemy, turning the lead of your fears and self-imposed limitations into the gold of your dreams and your destiny. Let it be.

Let it be. That's all I can do.

EVENING

Tomorrow has taken care of itself. My hosts have invited me to stay over again tomorrow night.

"It may not be the magic you seek, or even the magic you desire," I write in *The StarQuest*. "Magic knows none of that. Magic simply is." The same is true of miracles, and one more night free of a room charge and in the company of friends is definitely a miracle.

Day 73

Thursday, August 8
HAYWARD, CALIFORNIA

AFTERNOON

My Great Aunt Irene must be alive in whatever realm her will and estate reside because there was no hundred-grand deposit in my bank account overnight. But I did wake up to perhaps one of the most powerful songs ever written affirming infinite potential, Stephen Schwartz's "Defying Gravity" from the musical *Wicked*.

Although "Defying Gravity" is the perfect song with which to greet any new day, on this or any like journey, it's an unusually apt one for today, which in astrological and numerological circles is known as the Lion's Gate Portal.

I'm neither an astrologer nor a numerologist, so my intuitive take on this 8/8 day might be unorthodox. However, with the number 8 representing infinity (it's a sideways infinity symbol) as well as abundance, success and empowerment, and with lions representing personal power, self-confidence and courage, this is an ideal time to face down fear and self-imposed limitations and to activate the alchemy that transforms it into, as I noted yesterday, the "gold of your dreams and your destiny."

Given that my dream and destiny are pushing me farther out into the public realm with my voice and message (lion's roar), the fact that the Lion's Gate occurs in Leo (the energy of being in the limelight) is perfect for this stage of my journey. As an added bonus (and opportunity), my numerological destiny number is also an 8.

(Calculate your destiny number using the letters of your full name at birth; any numerology website will walk you through the process.)

Intriguing information, but how do I *feel* about all of this?

To be honest, I was a little shaky when I opened my eyes this morning, despite the uplifting song in my head. Today is the last of my three days of recharge and reflection here in Hayward. And if my sense of my "dream and destiny" has not altered — it feels stronger on this Lion's Gate day — I don't yet have any clarity on what my next step or destination ought to be. And without even a fraction of Great Aunt Irene's "legacy" and my copywriting job postponed until at least next week, my options feel more limited than unlimited.

Feel limited. In truth, my options are not at all limited. Only my perception is limited.

On the back cover of *The Voice of the Muse: Answering the Call to Write*, I promise that the book will transport you to "worlds beyond your conscious imagining." That phrase is singularly apt today. Our *conscious* imagination and perception are always limited by what we think we know and by what we have already seen and experienced. When we allow ourselves to open up to the realm that exists beyond that place of conscious imagining — in our lives as much as in our creativity — we move into the realm of infinite possibility, a realm that requires neither a Kula nor a Newport Coast to activate.

That realm is the realm of the heart...the realm of intuition...the realm of inner knowingness, inner vision and inner prophecy...the realm of our wisest self...the realm of infinite potential and infinite possibility.

The truth is that I don't need to know what I will do tomorrow, where I will go to do it or how I will pay for it. Of course, I would *like* to know. But that's different from needing to know.

All I need to know is that as wavery as it feels some days, my dream is still alive and my passion for it still burns white-hot.

As I've said before, this is not a dream of my personality mind, which would prefer a comfortable retreat far from the chaos and perceived dangers of the world. Nor is it some self-aggrandizing ego trip. It's an expression of my soul's yearning for its human form, and this human's interpretation of that yearning, which, as I have also noted previously, could possibly have lost something in the translation. For better or worse, this is the only translation I have to work with, so...

The sole path to any dream's realization (which is not an ending, merely a new beginning) exists step-by-step, moment-to-moment and breath-by-breath.

In this moment and on this breath, I am writing this because, for me, writing is a form of meditation. Like all forms of meditation, it calms me, centers me, keeps me in the moment and reminds me of my essential truth and beingness. In short, it clears my mind, reconnects me with the wisdom of my heart, opens me once again to my infinite potential...and helps me to defy gravity.

Day 74

Friday, August 9
Hayward, California

MORNING

After a three-day respite/recharge here, I'm packing up to hit the road again as the alchemy I wrote about the other day continues. My sights remain fixed on the LA area, but it's not time to return.

Not yet.

Soon.

For today, though, I don't know where I'm headed. On this journey of faith, all I can do is trust in the road my heart calls on me to take and in the miracles that will somehow find and sustain me.

One of those miracles found me yesterday: A twenty-dollar Best Western gift card that Best Western insists I've never used, even though I'm sure I have. In any event, it's now available toward a hotel stay.

May the miracles, each bigger and more magnificent than the last, keep showing up!

Anderson, CA
LATE AFTERNOON

Each time I woke up last night, and it was exhaustingly often, lyrics from "Defying Gravity" were singing in my head again. If I wasn't happy to be awakened at regular intervals, I could hardly complain about what greeted me each time. On a journey that teases me with endings that never come to pass and that dribbles out money and miracles on a drip feed, I'll take all the confirmation and validation I can get, especially when it's as potent as Elphaba singing about her unlimited future in *Wicked*.

This was the second day in a row that Stephen Schwartz's powerful lyrics reminded me of my infinite potential and of the infinite possibility that this regularly frustrating and often fear-filled odyssey represents. On a morning when I was set to leave the cocooning embrace of friends and relaunch myself onto the open road, it was extraordinarily welcome.

This afternoon, I'm in Anderson, with a little help from that twenty-dollar Best Western gift card. Mount Shasta is seventy-five miles or so north of here, and thanks to a few of those drip-feed miracles, I don't expect to have to sleep in my car up there. But although I petulantly (if unconvincingly, even to me) insisted that I wanted no part of any spiritual messages that might be waiting there for me when, in my fear, I initially selected Shasta as my next destination, that's clearly why I'm going.

From there, I expect to continue up to Portland and to stay no longer than it takes to pick up a few prescriptions and have coffee with my closest friend in the area. From there? Well, if I knew that, I wouldn't be living the day-by-day, moment-to-moment journey that I'm clearly meant to be living.

EVENING

I have experienced too much personal drama in recent days to devote more than a few random moments to my *Q'ntana* screenplay. Even in Hayward, I spent more time writing through my real-life SoCal-inspired PTSD then I did on fictional projects.

When I was working on it in bits and pieces at the Newport Coast Starbucks, I was writing in something of a vacuum. That's because I know less about this story than about anything I have written since the first draft of *The MoonQuest*, back in 1994-95.

All that changed as I walked Kyri up Balls Ferry Road a bit ago. As I headed toward Anderson River Park and the Sacramento River, it was as though the creative heavens burst open and the broad strokes of this fourth *Q'ntana* story rained down on me, more quickly than I could dictate them into Final Draft on my phone.

I'd like to think that all the trying times I have experienced recently are what opened the floodgates. At least it would give them some identifiable redeeming value. The fact is that however reluctant I am to admit it, those trying times already have their redeeming value, identifiable or not. And the *Q'ntana* story may have been waiting for this moment and place to reveal itself to me, regardless of recent events.

Still, I'm grateful, and I'm excited to start translating those notes into screenplay scenes.

Day 75

Saturday, August 10
ANDERSON, CALIFORNIA

MORNING

It's November 1997. I have been in Sedona since mid-September and in the US since early July. My six months as a legal visitor will expire in January, and I'm wondering whether to drive thirteen hundred miles to the nearest border crossing into Canada, wait a day on the other side, then turn around and return to start that six-month clock ticking again. I feel strongly, intuitively, that Sedona is where I need to be, but I'm not sure what to do about it.

In an attempt to get some clarity, I take off on a meditative hike among the red rocks of the Soldiers Pass Trail. As I listen for the still, small voice of my wisest self, I hear, *Don't leave. Stay in Sedona. Spirit knows immigration law.*

Spirit did, in fact, know immigration law. When it came time to apply for my green card less than a year later, the penalty for overstaying my legal welcome in those pre-9/11 times was minimal.

Spirit knows immigration law. That sentence popped back into my head this morning as I lay in bed worrying about an upcoming bill. Some bills you can delay paying; this one, probably not.

Immigration law, of course, is no longer an issue; I have been a US citizen for seven months. So that wasn't the point of the message. The point was to remind me that Spirit (aka my wisest self) knows all the intricacies of my situation, including the legally complicated ones and certainly the financially complicated ones, and that my sole job and responsibility is to listen and trust.

It's an ongoing reminder, and one that grows increasingly challenging as the stakes keep getting raised. My basic survival wasn't at play twenty-two years ago on that hiking trail, nor did it feel that way. And although it most likely isn't these days, it often feels that way.

It doesn't matter that not a single day has gone by when I couldn't eat (or feed Kyri), put gas in my car when necessary or find a decent bed for the night. There have been many days, though, when I wasn't sure I'd be able to manage all or some of that *tomorrow*. (Or make my car or insurance payment tomorrow or cover other perceived necessities tomorrow or…or…or…all tomorrow.)

I was having one of those days earlier this morning, hence the reminder.

It's more than a reminder to trust. It's a reminder to stay present in the moment. In the moment, at least on my journey, I have always been safe, I have always been taken care of, and I have always had (and been) enough.

When I can do more than believe that, when I can *know* it, there will no longer be any need to trust, nor will there be any new calls for faith. In most instances, both of those are forms of insurance: They make it feel possible to stay present in this moment, where everything is fine, by offering good odds that the next moments will also be fine.

So, really, my only job is *not* to listen and trust. My only job is to *be* — as fully present in each moment as I can, doing no more than what that moment demands of me (which could involve making plans for future moments, or even knowing what a future moment will bring, if that's what a particular moment demands).

The next moment is always Spirit's responsibility. And Spirit is always up for the task, even if I sometimes have a hard time trusting that. Because Spirit knows immigration law…and much, much more.

I do have a few hints of some of today's future moments, although they're subject to change. Once I leave Anderson, I will point the car toward Mount Shasta. Whether I'm able to get out onto the mountain will depend on the weather, which has not offered a particularly palatable forecast. From there, as I mentioned yesterday, I'll probably take a quick swing through Portland.

As for that bill and tonight's and future accommodation, they are not this moment's concern, as much as my mind tries to make them so. This moment's concern involves persuading Kyri to eat his breakfast. Then I'll pack, check out and try to let Day 75 unfold as it needs to.

Day 76

Sunday, August 11
MEDFORD, OREGON

MORNING

I woke up a little before three in Anderson yesterday morning wondering why my room was so dark and quiet and why I was so warm, until I discovered that the power had been knocked out by the night's storm. No AC, no sounds from the fridge in the room and no light leaking in from the motel parking lot. Perhaps I should have seen that as a sign that the day ahead could prove challenging.

It was. Writing my "Spirit knows immigration law" story helped dull the nonspecific anxiety I woke with. Unfortunately, it didn't dispel it. Then, to make matters worse, I accidentally drank about an eighth of a cup of hydrogen peroxide, not enough to do any damage but enough to give me heartburn and mild nausea. It was stupid to store peroxide in a water bottle and careless to pick up the wrong bottle when I was thirsty.

I suppose one could look at it symbolically, as part of the inner healing/cleansing journey I have been on these past eleven weeks. One could. I didn't. All I wanted was for the physical discomfort to go away. Then, I spent the next seven hours trying to make the emotional discomfort go away.

Sometimes, though, all we can do is free whatever needs to move through us to do so at its pace — be it peroxide or anxiety — and there is little we can do to speed up the process.

The drive up I-5 from Anderson, normally breathtakingly inspiring, felt drab and dreary in the off-and-on morning drizzle. There was a moment's promise when the sun burst through the clouds as I took the exit into Mount Shasta City. Alas, the promise evaporated five minutes later when I screwed up at one of the first traffic signals in town. With the red light still lit, a green turn light flashed on. My brain registered it as a full green, and I pushed through the intersection under the watchful eye of a traffic camera. I continued most of my way up the mountain, terrified that I would get a ticket that I couldn't afford to pay.

It was cold and blustery when I parked at the Bunny Flat trailhead twenty minutes later. I donned my fleece and hit the trail, hoping my presence on the mountain would settle and center me and open me to whatever intuitive guidance might be waiting for me up there.

Unfortunately, all I heard was rumbling thunder that threatened a storm at least as violent as the one that had cut power in Anderson the night before.

Frustrated and disappointed, I trekked back to the car. As I was getting Kyri settled, an incoming message pinged at me from my phone: KA'ryna, an old friend in Toronto, wanted to connect me with a friend of hers down in town. KA'ryna is a powerful intuitive, so I felt certain that anyone she felt guided to have me meet would be equally so. I immediately messaged Helen. But I was anxious to escape pricey Mount Shasta and get back on the road to somewhere more affordable, so I was relieved when she didn't respond right away.

Then, when I was partway down the mountain, she did respond. A short while later, I joined her at her house for tea. I hadn't taken more than a few sips before I realized that this was more a reunion than a new connection, and that spending this time together must have been why I felt called back to Mount Shasta.

Among the stories Helen shared with me was about a spiritual traveler of her acquaintance who had also been living on the edge with a dream. One day, out of nowhere, a stranger showed up with a sum of seed money to help her launch that dream. The gift was unconditional, and in an instant her life changed radically.

A mysterious benefactor has yet to materialize in my world. Yet I have had plenty of out-of-the-blue miracles over the years, where in an instant everything about my life changed for the better, in ways I could never have imagined.

It can happen again.

Today, I drive up to Portland for more closure with my former home. I'll be having a farewell coffee with my closest local friend, who's about to move away on an adventure of his own, and I'll be collecting my final batch of mail from my post office box. Until I land somewhere more permanent, I'm having my mail forwarded to Ted's in Hayward. So after today, with Blaine gone and no more mail to pick up, I'll have no reason to go back.

What happens after today? Will it then be time for Southern California? No idea. All I need to know is that I'm to continue on this path and allow the story, *my* story, to reveal itself to me, moment-to-moment.

Salem, Oregon
Late Evening

"Untethered." That's the best word I could think of to describe myself as I prepared to drive out of Portland this afternoon. On this, the seventy-sixth day since my exodus, I experienced another level of completion, perhaps the final one before I gain a new permanent address, somewhere.

In a way I didn't feel when I left Portland on May 28 or on either of my two lightning-quick returns to the city in the weeks since, I had been cut loose. The final cords connecting me with Portland had dissolved.

I felt untethered.

I'd like to say it felt liberating. It didn't. It felt scary. And as I sat in my car, uncertain where I would spend the night or in which direction I would travel tomorrow, I started to cry.

Freedom can be as scary as bondage. Freedom strips you of all certainty and all illusion of control. Freedom plunges you into the void of unknowingness. Freedom untethers you from all you have known and all you have been. Freedom hurls you into the lawlessness of your own personal Wild West.

Yes, freedom is exhilarating. It can also be terrifying.

Today, it was terrifying. I had finally lifted anchor — all the way this time — and I was now free to set sail for the promised land of my dreams. There was no turning back, and there was no guarantee that the seas ahead would be smooth. If anything, the guarantee was that they would be choppy.

It was already after four when I sat in my car, contemplating my next move. I had never left the search for a night's accommodation this late in the day. And I wasn't sure what to do or where to go.

I hadn't planned it this way. I had intended to get to Portland by one. Even with my errands and my quick coffee with Blaine, that would have left me plenty of time to intuit a direction, book a hotel and point my car toward the appropriate highway. However, checkout delays, gas station lineups, rest stops and freeway traffic all slowed me down. I didn't get into town until nearly three.

Now, it was late afternoon. Should I stick around or hit the road? If I hit the road, in which direction? I knew hotels in Portland and across the Columbia River in Vancouver, Washington wouldn't be cheap. But I had enough reward points for one free night with one of the chains. I opted to stay in the area.

The area didn't opt to have me stay. Or put another way, completion is completion, and closure is closure. The only pet-friendly vacancies I could find had pet fees that were pricier than some hotel rooms. I opted to leave.

Where to, then? North, west, east or south?

North would take me toward Seattle, likely more expensive than Portland.

West would take me toward the Oregon coast in high season. Also not cheap.

East along the Columbia? I was unlikely to find properties along that route that would take my reward points.

South, then…which is how I now find myself in Salem, about an hour from my old Pearl District neighborhood.

Does that mean I'm making my way back toward Southern California less than a week after having left? With what? My financial situation is tenuous enough that I doubt I can make it all the way there, let alone stay.

Still, how many times through these seventy-six days have I been certain that I was about to run out of money, only for one miracle or another to ensure that I didn't?

Then, there was this morning's experience at my Medford hotel. When I went to check out, there was no one at the front desk. While I waited, I noticed two business card stands off to the left; one held the cards for "Beverly Hills, operations manager." As I've mentioned here before, I have a history of Beverly Hills synchronicities over the years, all of which have pointed me toward that affluent Southern California municipality. Was this hotel's operations managers' unusual name another?

I still feel pulled to LA, even as the scale and scope of the miracle required for it to play out as my vision demands is beyond my imaginative capacity. Yet nearly every way my life has played out over the past three decades has also been beyond my imaginative capacity.

For now, I will remain open to the smaller miracles that keep me going from one day to the next and that help keep the dream alive, while striving to surrender unconditionally to the larger ones that I know deep down are always possible.

Meantime, if I am truly traveling moment-to-moment, I needn't know anything about LA or about tomorrow. All I need to know is that I'm in Salem tonight. And if in the morning, I continue to be pulled southward, that's where I'll go.

As my newly untethered self drove out of Portland this afternoon, I played and replayed Idina Menzel's Las Vegas performance of "Defying Gravity." If Elphaba's future is unlimited, mine can be, too.

Day 77

Monday, August 12
SALEM, OREGON

MORNING

On this, the final morning of my eleventh week of this personal odyssey, something has changed within me, as Elphaba sings in the opening line of "Defying Gravity." I'm not sure what it is any more than she is. But I do know that this leap I am about to take this morning is at least as big as hers, which makes an ability to defy gravity that much more important.

Barring any change in inner direction, my outer direction for the day is toward Los Angeles. A few weeks ago in Kingman, in a similar situation, I could not make the choice I am making today, even as my financial situation wasn't as challenging as it is right now. Instead of driving west into California, I drove north into Nevada. It was the first time in more than three decades that I had heard a clear intuitive call and ignored it. For all the pain that decision caused me, I was too scared to do otherwise.

I'm scared today, too. Terrified. As I wrote last night, the scale and scope of the miracles required to get me to LA and keep me there are so far beyond my mind's capacity to imagine that they must be impossible. Forget the big miracles. In this moment, my mind is struggling to figure out the small ones that will keep me on the road for the next few days…that will get a roof over my head tonight. To my mind, these, too, are impossible.

As I write these words, an inner chorus is singing the same "Defying Gravity" lyric about an unlimited future that I woke to a few mornings ago, reminding me why I'm here…reminding me to keep the faith.

Somehow, I have to find the strength to do that.

Day 78

Tuesday, August 13
ASHLAND, OREGON

MORNING

In a few hours, I drive into California. It is the first day of Week 12 of this Fool's Journey and will be my fifth foray into the state in that time. And what a journey it has been!

Yesterday morning, though, it was hard to believe that this odyssey could continue much beyond Salem. Temporary authorizations that had not yet fallen away had maxed out my one available credit card, and my meager Social Security deposit was late.

After breakfast, I sat on a park bench near the hotel and did an online search for places where it could be safe and acceptable to sleep in my car. National Forest land? Freeway rest stops? Walmart parking lots? Was living out of my car the next inevitable tumble on a financial tailspin that had kicked off in January, expelled me from Portland in May and kept me on a downward-trending roller coaster ever since?

When I finally sought inner guidance on the subject, the answer I got was unequivocal: *Don't even consider sleeping in your car.*

The next hours were filled with doubt that I tried to ease by listening to "Defying Gravity," along with some other songs that have lifted my spirits in the past. Later, during a picnic lunch in Eugene's Alton Baker Park, a succession of wasps interrupted my meal to remind me that "all things are possible" and that I deserve to have my dreams come true, at least according to the Spirit

Animal Totems website[4]. A few hours afterward at the Cabin Creek rest stop, a doe and her fawn reminded me, with a little help from a different website[5], of my strong intuition and my ability to handle challenges with grace.

Only then could I muster the courage to look for a room for the night or, more accurately, to commit to spending any of my seemingly limited resources on accommodation. After weighing the options, I settled on Ashland. My first phone call netted me a minor miracle: an affordable pet-friendly room. Every other time through the years that I have tried to stay in Ashland with a dog, pet-friendly hotel rooms have been scarce; affordable ones, non-existent.

As the freeway wound up and down the mountains of central and southern Oregon, my energy and mood improved. Instead of being frightened by the prospect of returning to California, I was excited. And for the first time since leaving Portland, I felt as though my life was primed for some radical and revolutionary *positive* change, and that the transformation was directly linked to my crossing the state line into California.

No matter what I asked and how I asked it, all answers pointed in the same direction: that once I was in California, I would feel, see and experience *real* improvement in all aspects of my life, including my finances. Suddenly, I noticed the music playing in the car. It was Barbra Streisand singing the title lines from "Happy Days Are Here Again." A few minutes later, it was Judy Garland singing "Lucky Day."

Were happy days about to be here again? Could this be my lucky day?

Later, as I took Kyri for his last walk of the night under the nearly full southern Oregon moon, I heard myself say, "This is the final day of my old life. Tomorrow, everything changes."

"For the objectively better?" I asked cautiously. "In terms I would

---

4. http://www.spirit-animals.com/wasp/

5. http://www.spiritanimal.info/deer-spirit-animal

immediately recognize as better from my human perspective?" The answer appeared to be yes.

Just before I turned out the lights last night, I saw a Facebook post announcing that the road up to Mount Shasta's Old Ski Bowl trailhead had opened that morning for its short summer season. Another sign? Maybe these seventy-seven days had truly been leading up to something magnificent whose time was finally on the cusp of arriving. "Please," I prayed aloud as I shut my eyes, "make it so."

It is now Tuesday morning and I'm lying in bed, trying to push through and past my anxiety that last night's optimism was false and that today and coming days would prove my intuition to have been a sham.

It's hard to shake the feeling that I'm seriously delusional. Last night's dream isn't helping. As the dream opens, I get two unexpected coaching gigs. That would be powerful validation, except that both clients stiff me for the fee. Meantime, my Social Security is still MIA, leaving me practically penniless as I gear up to step into this new life that allegedly begins today.

The key, of course, is that this new life is set to begin in California, where I'll be in a few hours, not in Oregon, where I lie in bed stressing.

So I guess I'd better get up and get moving and do what I can to remain hopeful and optimistic. At this stage of the journey, there's not much else I can do.

Anderson, California
Dusk

As Day 78 draws to a close, I'm still standing. Staggering shakily much of the time, but still standing. I can't write anything other than that. More later...

EVENING

I'm exhausted. Not physically, not mostly. Emotionally. Worn down and worn out. Throughout this journey, I have often spent my evening writing about my experiences. Nearly always, I have felt better for it.

Tonight, I can't. Instead, I'm sitting up in bed watching old episodes of the 1990s sitcom *Love & War* on my iPad and doing my best to not think about tomorrow and the day after that and the day after that. I have other writing projects I could be working on. Tons of them. They all feel futile. Everything feels futile. I feel futile. If I haven't lost all hope, I'm close.

If I can't trust my intuition, if I can't trust my inner knowing and wisest-self guidance, where am I? I crossed into California hours ago and *nothing* has changed. Happy days aren't here again, this isn't my lucky day, and everything is as fucked up as it was this morning.

What if everything I have intuited about this journey, including starting it, has been wrong? What if I am running myself into the ground and will lose everything? Any objective observer would come to that conclusion. Some of those who are following my so-called progress on Facebook have already suggested as much.

I don't know what to trust and believe anymore…if anything. And if I have gotten it all wrong, I'm at a loss as to how to fix it. Doesn't matter. It's probably too late to fix it.

A little voice inside me keeps whispering that everything's going to be all right. On whose terms? According to what definition?

I'm afraid to go to sleep tonight because I'm afraid it will speed me into morning and the need to make a decision about what to do next, about where to go next.

A week ago — a week ago today — I swore I wouldn't go back to LA, at least not without a substantial treasure chest. Now, I'm to go back with less than I had when I left? Am I doing the same thing over and over and expecting a different outcome? Isn't that the definition of insanity?

I sure feel insane. More than that, I feel lost, alone and, yes, abandoned. Sure, the pieces fell into place magically for me to get this room tonight. In doing so, however, they wiped out all but a few dollars of my available credit. What about tomorrow night?

Have I not given up enough, let go enough, stripped down enough?

I don't know what else to write or do until bedtime. I guess I'll watch another episode of *Love & War* and call it a night. Maybe my faith in tiny miracles hasn't dimmed. I'm not sure. It doesn't matter, though, because I've lost faith in the big ones. And only big ones can save me now.

Day 80

Thursday, August 15
GOLD RIVER, CALIFORNIA

EVENING

When I walked out of the Umpqua Bank in Red Bluff, California yesterday morning, I kept hearing the word I used here a few days ago: untethered. I had gone in to close my Portland bank account, something I couldn't do when I'd been in the city on Sunday when all branches were shut.

Umpqua was never my primary bank, and I rarely kept more than a few dollars in my account there. Like my post office box, however, it was a link in the chain that bound me to my life in Portland. Closing it shattered one of the final links in that chain. Closing it in person, even if I couldn't do it in Oregon, felt singularly significant.

As I walked back to the car clutching my two-dollar Umpqua bank balance, I felt unsteady, as though the world of my past had nearly faded into oblivion but the world of my future was not yet solid. Other than legalistic necessities, nothing of consequence now tied me to Portland. Yet not only had I not landed in California, I had no idea when, how or if it might be possible.

What had happened to the monumental shift in my life and circumstances that was supposed to kick in when I crossed the California state line on Tuesday? All I had to show for it was this pair of dollar bills, freshly liberated from my Oregon past — hardly the foundation for a new life of plenty.

Mount Shasta was the one bright light of my arrival in California on Tuesday. My morning dread had evaporated by the time I arrived, and after lunch in town with Helen, I drove up the mountain. As I made my way up to the top of the road, which ended at 7,840 feet, I was struck by the symbolism of my ascent: At a time in my life when I was feeling called to rise to my highest potential, I was climbing one of the highest-elevation paved roads in the state, a road that hadn't been open on my previous visits...that hadn't opened until the day before.

No new messages were waiting for me at what felt like the top of the world. That didn't matter. Up there, I had that same sense of infinite possibility I've so often experienced while sitting at the Newport Coast Starbucks, and it felt as though all I had intuited about my dreams and destination was being confirmed. Moreover, the one person I chatted with on the hiking trail was from Santa Monica, which, if you're familiar with LA geography, is adjacent to Beverly Hills.

Unfortunately, like the Kula effect I described two weeks ago, my euphoria didn't survive the drive back down. By the time I hit I-5 and pointed the car south toward Anderson, my mood had plummeted. And as I walked Kyri along the Sacramento River some hours later, I was certain that not only was I sliding into serious homelessness but that the best solution, contrary to all inner guidance, was to return to Mount Shasta in the morning and park myself in my car, indefinitely.

I didn't do it. Instead, I continued south toward Red Bluff and Umpqua Bank, and reflected on my time on Mount Shasta. My *times* on my Mount Shasta. It was on my initial post-Portland visit in late June that I first sensed a reawakened call to be in LA.

In the weeks since, I have been spiraling through the intense and profoundly alchemical process I described here a few days ago: turning the lead of my fears and self-imposed limitations into the gold of my dreams and destiny. Another way of looking at it could be a snake shedding old skin after old skin after old skin to get to its essence. A more apt metaphor, given the many hundreds of monarch butterflies I encountered on my Shasta-heights hike on Tuesday (Mount Shasta is on their migration route), would be a caterpillar-turned-butterfly pushing painfully against its cocoon in order to fly free and soar into the heavens.

After Red Bluff, I passed through Chico to do some errands. It was while there that I decided to book a room for the night in Jackson, a small wine-country town in the hills southeast of Sacramento. There was some logic to my choice: If I was going to continue vaguely south, it made sense to bypass the pricey Bay Area, and Jackson was more affordable than Sacramento. At twelve hundred feet, Jackson would also be considerably cooler than Chico or Sacramento.

As I drove through the town of Wheatland on my way, I passed a realtor's office. "We can make your dreams a reality," a banner in the window screamed. It was 3:33. Soon after, I had a call from Sacramento inquiring about a coaching session. I closed the deal by offering to do it in person on Friday, which is why I'm in Gold River tonight, in suburban Sacramento. That coaching gig is also how I will be able to limp through the next couple of days. If it expands into more than a single session, I'll be able to do more than limp. Fingers crossed.

I worried last night, as I was walking Kyri through Jackson and before the coaching session was confirmed, that my standard rates might be too high for this client, who would be booking it for his daughter. Should I have lowered them? Should I have discounted them? Should I have offered some other incentive?

"No," I heard myself say. "He's going to want the best for his daughter, and I'm the best." I was stunned. I had never described myself in those terms, had never dared describe myself in those terms.

Later in the night, I dreamt I was being asked to describe "who I am." Before I could answer, I morphed into an un-armored knight on a silver stallion, and a plume of white light rocketed me into the sky. In the dream, it was a rock that asked the question, a foundation rock that was keeping me grounded in the midst of my ascent.

When I woke up this morning, I felt that the dream had validated my sense that this journey is carrying me to great things. As challenging as it is so many days to believe it, I have to. I have to believe that I am already defying gravity. I have to believe…I have to *know* that I'm not on some random descent into disaster but on a powerfully guided journey into a fuller realization of my potential.

Continuing on this path takes more courage than many days I think I have. Somehow, I have to keep tapping into it. I have to keep staying open to the miracles. Because they're happening. Every day.

Gold River, CA
LATE EVENING

This message just in from a Facebook friend: "I've been speaking of you in quite a few conversations. Your choices moment-to-moment ripple far wider than you can possibly appreciate." I'll take all the validation I can get.

Day 81

Friday, August 16
FOLSOM, CALIFORNIA

LATE EVENING

It's February 1999. My then-wife and I have been on the Big Island of Hawaii only a few days, having left Sedona to follow the call of our hearts to the Land of Aloha. A few minutes before midnight, light sleeper that I am, I'm awakened by a crawling sensation on my shoulder. Reflexively, I brush it away, then scream in pain. I have been initiated to island life by a centipede and, according to poison control, there's nothing to be done, other than to take painkillers until the worst of the effect wears off by itself.

I don't know what bit or stung me a few minutes before midnight last night. Whatever it was left a red welt on my right knuckle before it woke me up. I leapt out of bed, switched on a light, grabbed Kyri and pulled the covers back. As in our Honaunau B&B all those years ago, the culprit had fled. Unlike in Honaunau all those years ago, I wasn't in excruciating pain, so it wasn't a centipede.

I was still alarmed. It could be hanging around to strike again. (That's what happened in Hawaii.) And it could be harmful to Kyri, even if it wasn't to me.

I debated calling the front desk. Would they take me seriously? Would they conduct an all-out search of the room? (The search in Honaunau had proven futile. The miscreant had fled.)

In the end, more out of concern for Kyri, I called. Whether he believed me or not, the night manager made sympathetic noises and offered to move me to an adjoining room.

When you travel like a turtle, with your entire life jammed into your shell, you carry more than an overnight bag and toiletries into a hotel room. And when you travel with a dog, there's even more to lug in from the car. But choosing caution over expediency and pajama-clad, I hauled all my stuff to the new room.

This morning, when I mentioned the incident to the regular manager, who, it turns out, is also the franchise owner, he said he wouldn't charge me for the night if I left his hotel immediately. Then, to my astonishment, he called me a liar. "I don't believe your story," he snarled. "No one here believes your story."

Twenty minutes later, I was packed and back in the car, anxiously scrolling through hotel apps on my phone to find something suitable nearby. I was counting on the proceeds from this evening's in-person coaching session, so leaving the area wasn't practical.

A half-dozen phone calls later, I landed five miles away in a room that is not only larger and more attractively appointed, it's a few dollars cheaper because the lobby and breakfast room are closed for renovation and the hotel's main entrance has been temporarily shifted to a side door.

More significant, I hope, is the key card: Spelled out in large, bold, upper-case lettering across the front is the word "thrive." Is this where my situation finally turns around? Is this where struggle disappears and easy flow kicks in?

And where does last night's episode fit into the equation? In Hawaii, the centipede bite presaged a series of setbacks that forced me into a job I hated and triggered the most serious crisis of faith I had until then ever experienced. Here, the setbacks have already occurred and my *crises* of faith far outstrip those of two decades ago. If the Big Island bite was the starting pistol for a race to the bottom, could last night's have been the starting gun for a race back up to the top? To a place where I can do more than barely survive? To the "gold of my dreams and my destiny"?

My "thrive" room key is propped up in front of me as I type this... in hope.

Day 82

Saturday, August 17
Folsom, California

LATE EVENING

I woke up before five this morning with my version of an anxiety attack. Nothing that would be medically diagnosed as such, but my chest was tight, my breathing was far from relaxed and my mind was on fear-filled overdrive. I never got back to sleep.

Once again, I was nearly out of cash and credit, and the "Defying Gravity" lyric playing in my head when I woke up felt like cruel mockery. Unlimited? Whatever the future might bring, my present felt *very* limited.

The few dollars I had transferred from PayPal to my bank account were in in-transit limbo, as were credit card funds that ought to have been available. Instead, they were locked in "pending hell." Both issues would probably resolve themselves in a couple of days. That wouldn't help me today.

Also in limbo was a freelance writing gig. It wasn't going to pay much. Still, it would pay *something*...once the client sent me the background material that would enable me to crank out the required short video scripts. But when would he send it?

As for the coaching-gig miracle that had brought me to suburban Sacramento two days ago, it had run its course. The good news for my writer-client is that all she needed was a single session to get her on track and launched. Although that kind of success is always immensely gratifying to the coach in me, the struggling journeyer in me had hoped she would need ongoing help.

I lay in bed, paralyzed with fear. Where would I go today? More importantly, where would I sleep tonight? No answers came.

I finally dragged myself out of bed at first light. Kyri needed to go out, and I needed to eat. Once breakfast was done, all I could manage was to go back to bed. I lay there for an hour, grasping for a solution that made some sort of sense. Problem was, I couldn't figure out how I could afford to move forward, yet I had no "back" to go back to, even if I could afford one.

I stayed in bed until nearly checkout time, hoping for some last-minute miracle to magically manifest.

None did.

Not for the first time on this journey, I felt angry and betrayed. Had all the inner guidance that I had followed to this point culminated in me being stripped bare? There was no way I could continue south toward LA, despite the ongoing urgings of my inner guidance.

"To hell with my inner guidance," I muttered. I had reached the limits of my faith, and I refused to use what few resources remained to me on what was undoubtedly a futile, beyond-foolish leap into disaster.

The one destination that made any sense to my overstressed mind was, again, Mount Shasta. It was cooler there (temperatures in the Sacramento area had been over a hundred for days), and I could sleep in my car there without being hassled. I packed up the Prius, topped up my gas tank and headed toward northbound I-5, even as that still, small inner voice predicted that I wouldn't make it all the way.

For the best part of an hour, I cursed, complained, blamed and second-guessed. I revisited every decision I had ever made that had brought me to this moment. I questioned every word I had ever written and every piece of counsel I had ever given. I felt like shit. In a moment of despair, I wondered whether I ought to seek a new home for Kyri in Mount Shasta. Given the uncertainty of my life and future, wouldn't that be the most humane thing to do?

Then, with my music collection streaming randomly through the car stereo, Andrea Bocelli burst into the Christmas song "God

Bless Us Everyone." I was about to skip it when a single word caught my attention: miracle. I restarted the track, and the instant Bocelli sang that the Christmas miracle had just begun, I experienced my own miracle: A notification popped up on my phone; I had received money. Not enough to get me to LA, but enough to get me a bed for the night and start me toward another one tomorrow. I wouldn't have to sleep in my car after all.

I burst into tears. I sobbed so long and so hard that I had to pull off the freeway. When I composed myself and checked the map, I noticed that I was halfway between Anderson, where I had spent the night on two previous trips to Mount Shasta, and Folsom, where I spent last night. Should I continue north or turn around and return south?

My fear screamed *NORTH*. I took a deep breath, reassured that terrified part of me and turned back. I would return to Folsom, to the same thrive-key hotel I stayed in last night.

I don't know where I'll go tomorrow. Given that there's no reason to stick around the Sacramento area another day, I hope I can summon the faith and courage to continue south, however indirectly.

Even in the midst of my terror today, even in the midst of my despair and peevish denials, I knew that that's where my dreams live. I knew, too, that if I can somehow keep believing in them, that that's also where I will find the miracles to make those dreams possible. That knowingness may always be present; unfortunately, it's not always easy to access...especially on days like today.

On days like today, it's also hard for me to recognize and acknowledge my courage and strength. On days like today, I feel anything but courageous and anything but strong. So I'm grateful to the friend who, in the midst of my angst this afternoon, acknowledged it for me. "You are profoundly courageous," she wrote. "It's very beautiful."

Day 83

Sunday, August 18
Folsom, California

MORNING

"I don't know what I will do tomorrow, and I am doing my best to be OK with that," I texted a friend last night.

"None of us does, truly," she wrote back. "We just make plans while Life does what it does."

It's true. We spend most of our lives living in the illusion of certainty, when the reality is anything but certain.

Who among us has not had our complacency shattered by a sudden illness, an unexpected death, a financial collapse, a relationship breakup or a natural or unnatural disaster? One day, we have a job, a paycheck, a home, a family, a life. The next, with no warning, one or all of those is snatched away. Did we ever have certainty? Or did we merely think we did?

Of course, our certainty need not be blasted to smithereens by bad news. An unexpected opportunity, a financial windfall, an unplanned (if welcome) pregnancy or a first date or random encounter that morphs into love at first sight: These can destroy the certainty of our status quo with equal ferocity.

Thing is, we expect certainty. We are almost wired to do so. A feeling of certainty helps us feel safe, keeps our stress at manageable levels, frees us to plan for the future. It's why our ancestors chose the caves they did, built forts and castles and invented insurance, pension plans and extended warranties.

My friend's text didn't tell me anything I didn't already know.

After all, the English language (and other languages, too, probably) is filled with aphorisms that speak to the illusion of certainty. "Man proposes; God disposes." "The best laid schemes o' mice an' men / Gang aft a-gley." "Better the devil you know than the devil you don't."

What does any of this have to do with this Fool's Journey of mine, now a few waking hours into its eighty-third day? If nothing else, this journey has been a potent exercise in shattering the illusion of surface certainties. Although I have traveled before without knowing where I was going from one day to the next, even for extended periods, I have never had to live so fully in the uncertainty of not knowing where my next dollar was coming from, when it was coming, or how I would manage a decent bed for the night. And only rarely have sufficient resources shown up to let me plan for more than a night or two in any one place.

I say "surface" certainties are being shattered because what I am experiencing more radically and intensely than at any other time in my life is where *true* certainty lies. It doesn't lie in externals like credit scores, bank accounts, available credit, fixed incomes and fixed addresses. True certainty lies within. It arises moment-to-moment from the still, small voice within us that knows no fear and thus needs no plans. Whatever you call it, it's the voice of pure love, an omniscient voice that transcends but never belittles the limited and limiting "common-sense" voice of the ego mind. It is the place of magic and miracles. It is the place where the only certainty of enduring value resides. It is only that certainty that can keep us safe, whatever life throws at us.

That's all great in theory, of course, and few people of a spiritual bent would disagree with any of it. Most, in fact, have put it into practice in some form, as had I before setting out on this journey... before being thrust onto this journey.

Until now, though, I had never been forced to live from that place of inner certainty so deeply and so completely. I had never been forced to trust it so absolutely. I had never been called to live it so fully.

It's clear from this chronicle that I don't trust it absolutely. If I did, I wouldn't have experienced the fear, anger and anxiety I have often written about. If I did, perhaps I would no longer be human. Even the biblical, altogether-human Jesus railed against God when he thought he had been abandoned.

My journey of faith — not in some external god but in the infinite wisdom of my deepest heart — is an ongoing one, carrying me (rarely fearlessly and not always gracefully) from one act of surrender to the next, from one trusting (or not-so-trusting) moment to the next, from one experience of *true* certainty to the next.

As for today, a few overnight miracles have ensured that I'm all right until tomorrow. And then? To borrow from last night's text: I don't know what I will do, and I am doing my best to be OK with that.

For now, I will once again pack up my gear, pack up my dog, pack up my car, top up my gas tank and take off, probably in a vaguely southerly direction, grateful for Kyri, grateful for the unending gifts and miracles of this journey and grateful for all the love, support and encouragement that has come my way.

Day 84

Monday, August 19
Patterson, California

LATE EVENING

When Kyri was rescued off the streets of Modesto, California last year, he was taken by Portland's Agave Dogs Rescue to Monte Vista Small Animal Hospital in nearby Turlock. So when I found myself less than an hour away from Turlock this morning, it felt right to bring him into the clinic to show him off.

I didn't expect anyone there to remember him or him to remember the place, so I wasn't sure why I felt called to go...until I was nearly there. About fifteen minutes from the clinic, I panicked. What if Kyri hadn't been abandoned? What if he had been lost? What if his original owner happened to be in the vet's waiting room, recognized him and wanted him back?

I knew my fear was silly, that the odds of that happening were less than infinitesimal. Yet I couldn't help but be anxious, so anxious that I nearly turned around. I didn't, and the visit was such a non-event that I wondered afterward why I had bothered. It wasn't until later that I understood why it had been important for me to go.

It had been important precisely because of the fear I felt on the way: the fear of losing something...something precious. Of course, the fear proved groundless, as nearly all my fears have over the past twelve weeks.

Unfortunately, that realization didn't prevent my second panic of the day, which would kick in toward the end of the afternoon.

After Kyri and I left Monte Vista Small Animal Hospital, we

drove to a nearby park for a walk and picnic lunch. Before we hit the road again, I did what was often a postprandial exercise: my daily juggle of cash and credit, designed to determine whether I could shuffle enough money onto one card to pay for a place to spend the night. Although my juggling act made it possible to book a room for tonight, it also revealed an uncomfortable truth. Barring new miracles, I would wake up tomorrow morning having bought myself another day or two on this journey or finding myself with zero cash and zero credit.

That's because book purchases from my website this past weekend had yet to make their way into my bank account and because the authorization for my un-charged Gold River hotel room was still tying up one of my surviving credit cards. The story is more complicated, but the bottom line is that to get a bed for tonight, I would have to gamble that the bank deposit *will* show up in the morning and that the authorization will do more than fall away; that it won't be consumed by finance charges due to kick in overnight.

I held my breath, crossed my fingers and booked a room in Merced.

A few hours later, while wandering through the ranch, orchard and vineyard country east of Turlock, I was hit by an attack of the what-if's. *What if my gamble doesn't pay off? What if the deposit is still delayed? What if the authorization still shows as pending in the morning?* By then, my second-guessing was pointless. The cancellation deadline for tonight's booking had passed. All I could do was make my way to Merced and hope for the best.

I pulled in to the hotel around five this afternoon, and after waiting twenty minutes to check in, my gamble blew up in my face: The front desk clerk demanded a hundred-dollar refundable deposit that I didn't have (I had scraped together barely enough to cover room plus tax plus pet fee). It didn't matter that the deposit hadn't been disclosed on the hotel website; the clerk refused to waive it. "All hotels around here have the same policy," she insisted.

For the next half hour, I sat in the car in the hotel's parking lot trying to figure out what to do and where to go. In the end, I booked back into last night's Best Western.

I was in tears as I wove through the farm roads that would take me back to Patterson. People keep telling me how strong and courageous I am. I felt neither. I felt scared. Had I done anything more on this journey than take two steps back for each step forward? If I was making any kind of progress, I failed to see it. All I could see was that I was falling farther and farther behind. Maybe that's why, when I'd thought about the LA dream earlier in the day, it was as though I was looking at it through the wrong end of a telescope. It still felt real, but it had never seemed so distant.

As I pulled into the Best Western parking lot a few minutes after seven, I remembered my morning panic about Kyri. The outcome I had been fearing was so improbable as to be laughable. Could this new fear fall into that same category?

I would like to think that's true. I would like to think that despite my fears, I will be okay. I would like to think that, having never been abandoned before, I will not be abandoned now. I have to confess, though, that as I sit up in bed writing this, my faith is shaky. At the same time, I have to trust. I have to do more than trust. I have to *know*. I have to live Step #10 in *The Way of the Fool* and "embrace the mystery." As the affirmation linked to that step declares, I must "give up my need to know and allow myself to be guided in faith as the Fool that I am."

As I sobbed my way back to Patterson this evening, two songs randomly shuffled onto my car stereo, back-to-back. The lyrics don't matter; the titles say it all: "Reason to Believe" and "Rise Again."

I'm grateful for all the supportive feedback I get, feedback that helps give me a "reason to believe," helps me know that I *will* rise again…helps me believe that I *am* making a difference, and not only in my life. Here are two examples of that feedback, from earlier today — "I respect you so much for having the guts and the faith to take this journey" and "You are doing sacred work."

Day 85

Tuesday, August 20
PATTERSON, CALIFORNIA

MORNING

What a difference a night makes. If I fell asleep at least somewhat hopeful, I woke up this morning ready to call it quits. On this first day of my thirteenth week of this journey of faith, I have lost all faith.

The funds I wrote about last night, funds I hoped would be freed up by this morning, have yet to show up. The video script-writing job is still in limbo. And a bundle of hotel points that's coming to me, that could buy me another free night's accommodation, won't be available for at least another day or two. As pushed to the edge as I have been in other moments on this journey and in my life, I find myself this morning dangling by a sliver of a hangnail.

At other times and in other circumstances, it might have been possible for me to wait out these delays. Not today. That's why I drafted this notice and have already posted it to all my social media accounts...

> WANTED (needed, actually): Free (initially) room and board pretty much anywhere for one weary, tapped-out journeyer and (hopefully) his dog, starting as quickly as I can get there. Once installed, I will look for a job (pretty much any kind) and try to regroup and rebuild.

This course of action did not come to me in meditation or from any other form of "tuning in to my wisest self." When it was suggested by a Facebook friend in the cold-light-of-day moments after

I checked my bank and credit card accounts this morning and saw that timing had not been in my favor, I viewed it as the only viable option. As clear as I believe my inner guidance to be about "staying the course," the most minimal of resources required to do that are simply not present.

I am doing my best to not declare these past twelve weeks and all that has led up to them a massive, wrong-headed mistake, if not a total failure. (Perhaps Kyri knows something I don't, because as I was in the middle of dictating that last sentence into my phone, he jerked on his leash so hard I dropped the phone.)

It's hard to see them in any other way. I'm not angry or scared. Or maybe I'm too numb with shock to feel either. All I know is that I have let myself be boxed into such a tight corner that I can't see how to extricate myself. But whatever "this" is can't continue...and not because I don't want it to. It can't continue because, today, I see no way for it to continue.

I hope someone replies to my post before I have to check out in an hour, because it would be helpful to have a direction to head in when I leave Patterson. One way or another and in one direction or another, though, I will be leaving — Patterson and, barring any sudden change in my circumstances, this phase of my journey.

Anderson, California
EVENING

I'm too exhausted, physically and emotionally, to write much of anything tonight. The bad news is that no one has replied to my ad, which is why I find myself back in Anderson tonight. The good news is that, thanks to some last-minute miracles, I *am* in Anderson tonight, not sleeping in my car up on Mount Shasta.

Beyond that, my life is mostly filled with uncertainty. One of the few ongoing certainties is Kyri. He needs to go out for a walk, and I need one, too. So, together, we'll stroll into the Northern California sunset. And while he continues to assume that his needs will be met indefinitely, I will endeavor to trust that the same is true for me.

Day 86

Wednesday, August 21
ANDERSON, CALIFORNIA

MORNING

If all the variables upon which I have based today's juggling are accurate and if they all play out as I hope they will, money will be okay for the next couple of days…I think. Still, I'm too exhausted to celebrate. I'm so exhausted that I almost feel paralyzed. I don't know how much longer I can keep doing this. Sure, I've said that before. But this is Day 86. I've been at this for nearly three months, and there's no end in sight.

Maybe I should drive up to Mount Shasta, park myself somewhere in the woods and never emerge. But if I start up there, I probably won't make it all the way. I never do when I think I'm going there to sleep in the car.

I am beyond worn out — from the traveling, from the money anxiety, from not knowing how I'm going to manage from one day to the next, from not knowing how long this is going to go on or where it's going to take me, from everything about my life.

Miraculously this morning, LA doesn't feel as wrong-end-of-the-telescope as it has in recent days. I can't help wondering, though, whether that feeling is real. Is anything I'm sensing and intuiting real? Even if it is, I doubt I have the energy to go on long enough to find out. It's not about will anymore, it's not about fear anymore. I just feel wrecked.

Six Rivers National Forest, California
EVENING

It's 8:40 PM, and I'm sitting up in the car in a National Forest campground whose name I don't know, trying to decide whether to keep the windows open a crack and be attacked all night by mosquitoes or keep them shut and suffocate. There's at least one mosquito already buzzing around my head in here, so I guess it's windows closed to stop any of its friends from joining it. With any luck, it will suffocate before I do.

After all those days when I thought, wrongly, that I would be forced to sleep in my car, it has finally happened....not that I'm likely to be able to sleep. I can't push the seat back because of all the stuff packed in behind it, and no position I've tried is remotely comfortable.

I didn't plan to sleep in the car tonight. (I also didn't plan to sleep in a campground without paying. Unfortunately, the pay station is self-service/cash-only, I have no cash and the nearest ATM is more than thirty miles away.) But my options were limited. Not because I have no money. I have two credit cards that each has enough credit on it for a hotel room for tonight. In theory. Through a glitch that no customer service agent or supervisor can fix, however, none of that credit will be available until tomorrow...at the earliest. (It's the "at the earliest" that prevents me from waiting until midnight to drive into town in search of a hotel or motel. I'm out of cell range up here, so I will have no way finding out whether the funds have cleared.)

When I discovered all this, I was forty-five minutes from Eureka, the nearest town of any consequence, it was already dusk and this campground was the best bad option.

It's not that I mind sleeping in the car; after all, I was prepared to do it last night. I mind that it's too dark and buggy outside to eat dinner. I mind that it's too dark and buggy outside to try to move things around in the car in a way that might let me push my seat back. And, as I've already mentioned, I mind that it's too buggy inside to open the windows. Moreover, it's impossible to relax when a ranger could come by at any time and, given that I haven't paid and can't, insist I move on.

What a perfect end to this day...

I'd already packed up my stuff this morning when I was so overcome with exhaustion that I decided to lie down on the bed for a few minutes before loading the car. It wasn't physical exhaustion. It was emotional fatigue from the daily struggle to keep this journey going.

With my eyes shut, I murmured to whatever essence or energy might be listening, "Take me now. Make it quick and painless, and make sure Kyri's taken care of. Just do it."

I wasn't suicidal. I'm too concerned about a suicide's potential effect on my daughter to go through with it. And what would happen to Kyri, already twice-abandoned before he rescued me? Still, if in that instant I could have seen lightening about to strike me down, I doubt I would have tried to dodge it.

Instead of lightning, what I saw in mind's eye was a doorway opening to the light, a doorway that was very, very, *very* far away, likely signaling that my death is many years distant. "I guess I'm not going anywhere anytime soon," I muttered. I forced myself up, loaded the car and took off.

Had I aimed for Mount Shasta (and made it), yes, I would be sleeping in the car. But if I'd had daylight hours in which to prepare, I could have made myself more comfortable, and my stomach wouldn't be growling. Instead, I followed what I assumed to be my inner guidance and picked up CA-299 in Redding for a spectacular drive across the Mendocino Mountains toward the coast...only to find myself stuck in the midst of them tonight

I don't know what I'll do or where I'll go in the morning. It would be nice to think that I will be in a better frame of mind, that I will be more surrendered, or that a massive, magical miracle (and not a park ranger) will welcome me to Day 87. None of that (except, possibly, for the ranger) feels likely.

Day 87

Thursday, August 22
Six Rivers National Forest, California

MIDDLE OF THE NIGHT

It's now 1:10 AM. I've tried opening a window the tiniest of cracks. All that that's accomplished is to invite in more mosquitoes. It hasn't alleviated the stifling stuffiness.

I've tried nibbling what I can from just inside the cooler, but I'm not double-jointed enough to reach more than a few grapes and some crackers. I never had dinner, so I'm famished.

I've tried every position I can contort into, yet none has been comfortable enough to let me fall asleep.

I don't know what the new day will bring, but this is already proving to be an excruciatingly long night.

Burney Vista Point, California — Trinity Highway (CA-299)
DAWN

I made it through the night, managed to get a few hours of frequently interrupted sleep (though my neck and back may never be the same) and took off at first light...to avoid any rangers on dawn patrol.

I'm about five miles west of what I now know to be the East Fork Campground, back in cell range and grateful to learn that one of my credit cards has sorted itself out: The funds that should have been available last night but weren't, are now. Unfortunately, the other card is *still* waiting for that Gold River hotel manager to release the pending charge for last week's aborted stay. If he doesn't do it manually, my bank tells me, it could take up to thirty days for it to fall off on its own. The hotel chain's customer service department was sympathetic but unhelpful; I won't stay at one of their properties again.

As for today, I can't face retracing my steps back over the mountain; two and a half hours is a long way to Redding on an empty stomach. The coast is nearer; it's about forty-five minutes to Eureka. So I'll make my way there and, with any luck, have some sort of personal *eureka!* over breakfast.

I've lost count of the number of the times and ways I have tried to abort this journey and touch down somewhere...anywhere. My most recent failed attempt was with that (as-yet-unanswered) notice I posted two days ago from Patterson. Yet If I'm honest with myself, I have to admit that I'm going where I need to be going and doing what I need to be doing...even if it often makes no sense to my logical mind. That must include last night in the car, as impossibly uncomfortable as it was and as deeply pissed off as I originally was.

It was hard to trust last night, in much of anything. Still, I made it through, and I'm going to try to believe that last night's were the worst moments of this journey...that it gets easier from here.

Where does this Fool's Journey take me from here? I can't predict. I will predict what's immediately ahead, though: down the mountain to Eureka. Starbucks must be open by now, and I need coffee and food if the journey is to keep going...wherever.

So many people care about me and believe in me. Some even believe in this journey. I have no words to express how grateful I am for all the support and encouragement in all the ways it has shown up over the past nearly ninety days. Whether it's being cheered on or helped out financially, I could not have lasted this long without it.

RED BLUFF, CALIFORNIA
EVENING

I'm fine, I'm safe and I'm under a roof (not a car roof) tonight. I'm grateful for the bed. I'm considerably more grateful for the bathtub.

After I left the vista point this morning, I drove into Eureka for what turned out to be a miracle breakfast. It was a miracle because I got it for free. The Starbucks barista got so flustered punching in my order — I was paying for my Americano, but I was using reward points for my toasted bagel — that she comped my coffee to make up for the wait.

Afterward, still shaky from my night in the car, I made my way to Avenue of the Giants, which runs through the towering redwoods of Humboldt Redwoods State Park, thirtyish miles away. I figured that if anything could offer me the balm I needed, it was those wise titans. One picnic lunch and one meditative hike later, I hit the road again — refreshed, restored and ready to resume the journey...at least for now.

As it turned out, that journey carried me back through the mountains and dropped me here in Red Bluff. Ironically, I'm barely twenty miles south of Anderson, where I launched this chapter of my adventure only two days ago.

There's more to share, though not tonight. If Kyri will let me, I'm going to soak for a *long* time in my room's most welcome tub, then call it a night.

Day 88

Friday, August 23
Fremont, California

LATE EVENING

On those days when it feels impossible to trust, when I feel delusional to believe that these journeyings have a higher purpose, when I am desperate for the perceived insanity to stop, I am forced to remember the many miracles and synchronicities I have experienced through these eighty-eight days on the road.

Whether it's the Americano that yesterday's barista didn't charge me for or my presence at the same I-5 rest area on two separate occasions over the past week when, each time, I learned of a financial miracle that would prevent me from having to sleep in my car that night, I have been blessed by something hopeful and helpful on every day of this journey.

And each of those miracles has reminded me that, as I always have been, I am being taken care of, I am safe and, as hard as it can be to believe, I am on the right track.

Even when, two nights ago, a credit-card timing snafu forced me to spend the night in my car, there happened to be a National Forest campground up the road from where I was parked when I received the news. On top of that, I scored the last vacant campsite. Those weren't the miracles I was seeking. Still, they *were* miracles. It could have been worse. Much worse.

Tomorrow's miracle has already revealed itself: For the fourth time on this journey, I have been invited to Hayward for a few days' respite from the road. Without this journey, in all the uncomfortable ways it has played out, I would never have met Ted and Rich, my hosts there. What a gift! There have been so many others, including the deeper connections I have forged with online acquaintances I now view as friends.

Those gifts could never have materialized had I not let myself be as vulnerable as I have been in these writings. Of course, I have let myself be vulnerable in print before now. In one way or another, all my books are an expression of that. Yet there is a difference between reflecting on my "past nakedness" from the relative safety of the future and publicly sharing my raw emotions of the moment, as I have done with many of these posts.

I know those raw emotions have pushed buttons for some and have caused others to express serious concerns for my well-being. Yet I couldn't be true to the authentic writer I endeavor always to be if I were to censor myself. Nor could I be of assistance and inspiration to those who are going through or have gone through their version of my experiences were I to hold back.

These are intense times for many, regardless of one's spiritual bent or practice, or lack of either. I know some of you have felt so beaten up and beaten down by life that you have wished for a "permanent way out," even if you've wished it for only the briefest fraction-of-a-nanosecond instant (as I did the other morning, causing many of you understandable alarm). I shared my experience not to be sensationalist or exhibitionist and not to provoke pity, but to reassure those of you who have felt similarly that you're not alone.

In the end, I hope that's one of the things all my writing accomplishes: to reassure at least one of you that you are not alone, that you needn't be ashamed of feeling scared, that you needn't be afraid to acknowledge your fear, that your vulnerability is a strength, not a weakness, that your vulnerability is a sacred gift to the world, not a liability.

It's so easy to put up barriers and wear masks to hide who we truly are and what we truly feel. It feels safer to veil our innate brilliance...to arm and armor our hearts. Yet if, as Gandhi urged, we are to be the change we wish to see in the world, we must be in the world as we truly are, not as some sanitized Barbie- or Ken-doll facsimile.

It isn't always easy for me to write what I write and to share what I share. Part of me would prefer to live the twenty-first-century equivalent of a monk-scribe in a cave at the top of a mountain, preferably writing under a pen name. The world doesn't change, though, when we hide from it. The world changes only when we are fully (and, perhaps, Fool-ly) present in it — with our hearts exposed and our *perceived* faults and flaws visible to all. "Perceived" because, more often than not, those qualities are viewed as faults and flaws by no one but us.

"I feel naked," I wrote one day in the journaling that seemed to be pushing me to turn it into a book. It would ultimately become *Dialogues with the Divine: Encounters with My Wisest Self,* the book that contains some of my rawest, most vulnerable writing. "I feel exposed," I continued. "People will laugh. People will judge. People will destroy me, annihilate me."

The words that emerged from my wisest self in response were more terrifying: "Walk the earth naked, clothed only in your truth. Book or no book is not the issue. Coming out is the issue. Being out in the world with your truth is the issue."

This was not about coming out as a gay man. I had done that more than a decade earlier with minimal fallout. It was about coming out as frightened, vulnerable and imperfect. It was about coming out as human.

That is what I do strive to do daily as I chronicle my experiences on this journey. Yet I can't share my humanity unless I am prepared to *be* that humanity with its roller coaster ride of joy and grief, terror and triumph, crisis and courage. And I can't survive that roller coaster unless I open to the miracles that, as I put it in *The Way of the Fool,* "are at hand in every moment of every day."

The book's eleventh step, as I've mentioned before, is "Embrace the Magic," and what follows is an excerpt from that step's introduction.

"It's our limited vision that prevents us from seeing [those miracles]. It's our limited sense of what is possible that prevents us from believing in them. It's our fear that prevents us from embracing them.

"How do we attract more magic and more miracles into our lives?

"By opening our eyes, hearts and minds in awe and gratitude to the abundant miracles already magically present — from the miracles of breath, of laughter, of love, of life, to the magic of a flower, a rainbow, a seascape, a sunrise, to the miracles of serendipity, synchronicity, wonder, connection.

"It's not about 'expecting' miracles to show up. Expectation removes us from the now moment.

"Rather, it's about acknowledging what is already abundantly present in our field of vision, for it is our openness to everyday miracles that seeds the exceptional ones. And it is the exceptional ones that remind us that on the Way of the Fool, the impossible is always possible."

In the midst of the perilous-feeling roller coaster ride that is this odyssey I have been living for the past eighty-eight days, I have to believe that the impossible *is* always possible, especially on those days when even the possible feels absolutely impossible. If I didn't, as I've said here before, I couldn't keep going.

Day 89

Saturday, August 24
Hayward, California

LATE AFTERNOON

After my unexpected and uncomfortable night in the car Wednesday night, as I noted the other day, I followed US-101 south toward Humboldt State Park and Avenue of the Giants. As I expected from this, my fourth visit there since 1997, nature's redwood cathedral did much to revive my spirits and recharge my energy. I needed the womb-like embrace of those ancient and mighty trees before I could face this journey again, before I could face the world again.

I had three choices when I reached the end of Avenue of the Giants: return north along 101, perhaps all the way up into Oregon, continue south toward the Bay Area, also on 101, or cross back over the mountains to the open spaces along I-5. I didn't yet know I would be returning to Hayward.

I-5 won out.

The quickest way over the mountains would still be long: nearly four and a half hours, mostly on unnumbered back roads. What I couldn't see from the map was what those four and a half hours would be like. It took well over two hours along often-questionable roads (not highways) to travel barely one-third of the distance.

The roads were all paved, after a fashion. That's the best that can be said for most of them. In addition to their radical ups and downs, they were poorly maintained, with frequent crevasse-like potholes, rough gravely bits and one-lane stretches where chunks of the pavement had, literally, fallen off the mountain. Not surprisingly, the speed limit through part of the journey was a supersonic fifteen miles per hour.

A few miles before I turned off West Van Duzen Road onto CA-36, the pavement smoothed out, and for the first time in nearly three hours, the road sported a clearly painted center line. It may not have been a straight shot through to Red Bluff from there, but it was now a much easier drive.

Could this mini-journey over the mountains, I asked myself as the road evened out, be a metaphorical microcosm of the longer one I had been traveling since leaving Portland? If it was, where was I now situated?

Like my earliest days on the road, Thursday's mountainous trek started out deceptively smoothly, only to grow more circuitous and roller coaster-like soon after. That next bit, long in time but short in miles, seemed to last forever. And though I was never in any danger, it did have its harrowing moments.

Was I still navigating those steep grades, sharp curves and pocked roads in my life? Had my Fool's Journey begun to level out? Had I turned onto the CA-36 stretch yet, still long in miles but a cakewalk compared to what had preceded it?

I knew what I wanted my answer to be. After Wednesday night in the car, I longed to believe that I had left the worst behind me, that I had survived this journey's most challenging ordeals and that I was transitioning into the "smoother ride" stage.

Is that yearning moving into reality? In the days since, I have sensed that a turning point is imminent, perhaps as soon as this coming week, the beginning of my fourth month on the road. Is it finally time for some of those larger miracles to show up? If not the LA-related ones — for better or worse, Southern California doesn't feel imminent — then the financial ones...the ones that could give me a solid sense of purpose and direction.

Although not itself a miracle, this morning's phone conversation could be part of that shift, however indirectly.

I was relaxing on the patio of my Fremont hotel in the hours before checkout when Aalia, my ex-wife, called. She had a writing project she was eager for me to help her with, one that could potentially lead to a handsome financial payout.

"Come to Sedona," she urged. "We can work on it together." As added incentive, she offered to let me stay in her new condo until she moves into it next weekend. It will be empty, apart from an air mattress, a chair and a snack table. And it will be free.

I haven't decided. On one hand, the potential payout is probably a long shot. On the other, I have to go somewhere when I leave here on Monday...and free is free. On the third hand, there's the timing: This coming week will be three weeks shy of the twenty-second anniversary of my first Sedona landing, after a road odyssey (with a dog) that lasted about as long as this one has. Is that a coincidence or a sign?

I'll let that one steep for a bit.

Meantime, I'm eagerly anticipating thirty-six hours or so of respite from the stresses and challenges of my daily road routine. I plan to do as little as possible.

Day 91

Monday, August, 26
HAYWARD, CALIFORNIA

AFTERNOON

Yes, I'm still in Hayward. Ted and Rich invited me to stick around one more day, and I'm beyond grateful for the extended break — from the road as well as from the intensity of this past week. It has also given me more time to consider Aalia's offer.

I was already leaning toward accepting when she threw one more incentive at me: The owner of The Literate Lizard, the local bookshop, has agreed to let me host a writing class in her store next Sunday. To sweeten the pot, she won't take any cut of whatever fee I charge. Plus, I can sell my books there.

Of course, I said yes. Who could resist all that?

I'm excited about the possibility of teaching again. Wary, too. Of all the classes I tried to get off the ground in Portland, only one ever happened...and it wasn't much of a success, at least not in terms of attendance. It was the *Way of the Fool* class I facilitated at the New Renaissance Bookshop less than three weeks before my exodus, not yet knowing I would be leaving. It attracted two people, one of them my friend Blaine. I haven't taught a well-attended workshop since Albuquerque.

Regardless, it's worth a shot. So when I leave here tomorrow, it looks like I'll be pointing the car back toward Sedona.

Day 92

Tuesday, August 27
Barstow, California

EVENING

There's no way I can catalogue the insane number of synchronicities and other quirky serendipities surrounding my decision to return to Sedona tomorrow. All I can say is that there is a mind-boggling number of them, and more keep showing up.

Is Sedona where the shift in this journey and in my circumstances that I intuited last week kicks in? I guess I will find out in the next days. All I know for certain (which is not much) is that I sensed that things would begin to change tomorrow, and that's when I arrive back in Sedona — exactly three months from the day I left Portland.

What does all this mean? Not a clue. Will I be staying in Sedona? Not indefinitely. The LA thing hasn't gone away. At the same time, I'm open to sticking around for a while if it feels right and if there is a way to do it that makes some semblance of financial sense.

Tonight, as I sit up in my bed in Barstow, halfway to Sedona, I confess to a tiny amount of trepidation as I contemplate this return trip to my first US home. I have lived other places for longer periods (nearly everywhere) or through more concentrated intensity (Hawaii). But of all the places I have lived, Sedona (I have lived there twice) is where I have experienced the most revolutionary life changes, the most radical shifts in identity and the most joys and despair. If my fearful self worries about what mischief Sedona could have in store for me this time, I'm endeavoring to keep my focus instead on all the gifts that I trust are waiting for me there tomorrow.

For now, all I know is that after I pack up the car in the morning, I'll be following an all-too familiar route: east on I-40 to Flagstaff, then down the winding road through Oak Creek Canyon to Sedona.

Postscript: Of all the workshop topics that could have been requested for Sedona, the one I was asked to facilitate is the only one that had its origins there: "Birthing Your Book...Even If You Don't Know What It's About." That title began as a section in *The Voice of the Muse: Answering the Call to Write*, morphed into a workshop (last offered in Sedona a decade ago) and grew up to become an eponymous book of its own.

Day 93

Wednesday, August 28
Barstow, California

MORNING

Packed, checked out, ready to hit the road for Sedona and eager to embrace whatever magic and miracles it has in store for me.

Sedona, Arizona
LATE EVENING

I'm here. I'm not yet sure what it means to be here, not least because it has been a whirlwind since pulling into town late this afternoon. I have spent most of that time trying to remember to breathe.

I have passed through Sedona often since December 2004, the last time I lived here. This visit, though, feels different, much different even than my most recent overnight stay, six weeks ago.

First, I'm camped out in the guest room of the empty condo that my ex-wife doesn't occupy until this weekend. If that isn't strange enough, I will probably be here for a few more days after she moves in.

Like spending extensive time with my ex (for the first time in nearly twenty years without the presence of our daughter), being in Sedona feels at once intimately familiar and intensely alien.

In the four years I have lived here, separated into two segments by the three and a half I lived in Hawaii, I experienced what feels like dozens of lifetimes. Am I now on the cusp of another?

Long-distance driving is a form of meditation for me, and I have often used it, as I did yesterday, to put that time to creative use.

Other times, like today, I intuitively tune into what's going on in my life to feel out what's next. Yet, for all I tried yesterday and today, I failed to get a fix on what it means to be here or on the fate of the tentative and unfunded writing opportunity that enticed me here. Nor could I summon up any sense of how I might finance anything much beyond Sunday's workshop.

Sometimes, we are called to make a clear choice and allow the universe to respond accordingly. I don't think this is one of those times. Instead, I must stay open to all possibilities and let my story here unfold in whatever way it needs to…in whatever way I need it to.

There's a scene in *The MoonQuest* where the book's four main characters are shown two conflicting outcomes to their journey. "The truth has yet to be written," they're told. "It hangs, waiting — but not forever. Before another day passes Prithi will carve it into the earth. Then it will be fixed for all time."

Similarly, I sense that the truth of my time here in Sedona has not yet been written, that Prithi (the deity of my *Q'ntana* fantasy world) has not yet carved it into the earth.

I would like to be able to stay for a bit. I wasn't sure I'd be able to say that when I committed to coming for a few days. But as I drove down Oak Creek Canyon from Flagstaff late this afternoon, the thought of being here for longer — perhaps as long as a month or two — moved me to tears. Not because I would be off the road, but because I would be in the transformational energy of this sacred place. Because I would be back in one of my spiritual homes. Because I felt that I wouldn't be bruised and battered by its energy, as I have been, but embraced and supported by it, which I also have been.

All I can do for right now is be here. I will prepare for Sunday's writing workshop, I will throw together a flyer for it and post it around town, I will get out onto the trails with Kyri and I will remain open to whatever bundle of gifts Sedona has to offer me this time…for however long "this time" is meant to last.

And I will hope that the upward shift in my life and circumstances that, last week before I knew I was coming to Sedona, I intuited would kick in today, has truly been initiated.

Day 94

Thursday, August 29
SEDONA, ARIZONA

LATE EVENING

Twenty-one years, eleven months and eighteen days ago, I drove into Sedona for the first time. I arrived after eighty-eight days on the road with no plans to stay. After four days, in fact, I checked out of New Earth Lodge, ready to resume my journeying. I never did. Instead, I returned to the front desk, checked back in and didn't leave until three months later, when I moved into an unfurnished condo of my own.

Today, it's impossible not to notice that journey's similarities with this one, right down to my canine companion. Even the span of the two journeys is nearly identical. And although my starting points were practically a continent apart, this morning's experiences suggest that their end points were always destined to be the same.

Last night, I expressed uncertainty about whether I was to stay here much beyond Sunday's workshop. This morning, that uncertainty evaporated. Or, perhaps more accurately, certainty found *me* during a meditative hike along Sedona's Soldiers Pass Trail, the same trail where, in the closing weeks of 1997, I felt guided to not drive up to the Canadian border to restart the clock on my six-month visitor privileges. "Spirit knows immigration law," I heard.

I mentioned previously that I have lived in Sedona twice before. Of course, that means I have also moved away from Sedona twice. The first time, when my ex and I moved to Hawaii; the second, when our marriage broke up.

For all I have written and spoken over the years about my experiences getting here and living here, I have never delved into how it felt to leave. That changed early this morning. As Kyri and I clambered up the red rock trail, I was overcome by a profound sadness. That sadness had nothing to do with yesterday's return to town; it had everything to do with those two departures. Although I had experienced the full emotional impact of the life events that precipitated those leave-takings, until this morning I had never given myself permission to acknowledge how wrenching those leave-takings had been. This morning on that trail, I felt all the grief I had buried when I'd walked away from the spiritual oasis that the land here has always been to me. With each exodus, it was as though a part of my soul had been ripped out.

At the time, I couldn't let myself feel all that. How could I when on each of those occasions it was powerfully important for me to move on, for me to leave Sedona behind? I couldn't.

This morning, finally, I allowed myself to touch that anguish. Once I did, it was clear where my lingering resistance to landing here was coming from.

Are you prepared to surrender fully to Sedona, my wisest self asked, *knowing you might have to leave again?*

I desperately wanted to say no. How could I say yes and face that heartbreak again, a heartbreak I now knew to be nearly as intense as the one I had felt at the end of my marriage.

I hesitated. I knew I would have to say yes. I knew that this could only be another act of surrender in a lifetime filled with acts of surrender. I knew it, but I was hoping against hope that, in waiting, the question would change, that I would be encouraged to stay without the probability of having to leave again at some future date.

In the end, as I always do, I surrendered. "I will stay," I said aloud. "I will make this my home again for as long as it needs to be my home. And when the time comes, if the time comes, I will move on to whatever is next for me on this journey, be it LA or somewhere else."

I shared that story with several friends today. Each time I reached the part about how heartbreaking my previous departures from Sedona had been, I felt a surge of emotion and a flood of tears, an unassailable sign of its truth.

In June 2002, my wife and I had barely been back in Sedona from Hawaii for a week when we attended a Chamber of Commerce mixer at a local metaphysical center. As part of the cost of admission, we received a ticket for a free intuitive reading. Before turning over her tarot card, the reader, a stranger to us, looked up and said, "You're wondering if you're in the right place." She paused for an instant. "You are."

I felt that same surge of emotion and rush of tears when I shared this story, this time with my friend Joan, who arrived in Sedona in late 2004 as I was getting ready to leave. "You're in the right place," she said, echoing that long-ago reader.

I stopped behind a Toyota Camry at a traffic light this afternoon. Its license plate read "RITESPT." That rightness of this spot is already making itself known, in both minor and major ways.

- Last night I discovered that my America the Beautiful senior pass will let me park at all the area's trailheads for free. Normally, a paid Red Rock Pass is required at many of them. I had been granted a passport to Sedona.

- Though this weekend's workshop is a few days away, The Literate Lizard's owner has encouraged me to plan more events at her store. "You can do an event here anytime you want," she said, when she learned I'd be staying in town.

- When I hauled a banker's box filled with my books into the bookstore this morning for a pre-workshop display, the box self-destructed as I set it down. All the books tumbled onto the floor, as if shouting, "We're staying!"

- This morning, as I was walking to my car, having surrendered to staying, I declared aloud, "If I'm to stick around, I need a place to live." Within seconds, my phone pinged to an incoming text. It was from a longtime Sedona friend. "I have manifested an amazing place for you to stay," she wrote. Clients of hers have had to call off their trip to Sedona, too late to cancel their booking at Poco Diablo, a local timeshare. The unit, she said, is mine for the next three weeks starting tomorrow, if I want it. Better still, it's free. Do I want it? Hell, yes!

What's next? For the first time in what feels like a lifetime, I don't have to worry or wonder about where I'm going tomorrow or the day after that…or the week after that…or the week after that. Unless Sedona has second thoughts, or I do, I'm here until September 26; probably beyond.

As in 1997, this is an unexpected and unpredictable outcome. I never planned to return to Sedona and, once here, didn't plan to stay. Yet here I am. I can't know what the future holds but, for now, it looks like I'm here. Living in Sedona. Again.

The Fool's Journey recounted here may be over, but this Fool's journey continues. As M'nor tells Toshar in The MoonQuest, *"There is no end to the quest for those who choose to live the journey."*

Afterword

Remember who you are.
The Way of the Fool

You enter into this lifetime in the leap of faith
your soul takes into the being in your mother's womb.
You take that one huge leap only to discover that
such leaps never cease being demanded of you.
The Voice of the Muse: Answering the Call to Write

Two years later, I'm still living in Sedona and still living the new chapter on this Fool's Journey that began when I drove into town in the final days of August 2019. If that isn't strange enough, and sometimes it feels mighty strange, my home is five doors down from that first condo I rented in 1997 when I moved out of New Earth Lodge. Stranger are the moments when it's as though I never left at all.

As I intuited it would in the days after overnighting in the car in the Northern California mountains, my life did change radically, almost immediately, and not simply because I was off the road. Free accommodation at Poco Diablo wasn't the sole miracle with which Sedona blessed me in those early months. Four more housing miracles followed that one, including the one that dropped me here in my old neighborhood twenty-one months ago.

The most dramatic of all the miracles, however, was the one that made it possible for me to support myself again.

A few weeks after that initial class at The Literate Lizard, I launched a regular series of writing workshops at the bookstore. Not only did that boost my book sales, it gained me a full roster of coaching clients. It was those coaching sessions that gifted me with the most financial stability I'd enjoyed since leaving Albuquerque for Portland.

And my creativity was in full flow. Resuming a project I had initiated in Portland, I published new editions of eight of my books, including a vastly expanded version of *The Voice of the Muse: Answering the Call to Write*. I also returned to *The Bard of Bryn Doon*, folding those early screenplay scenes into a novel, which came out a few days before I started work on *Pilgrimage*.

Pilgrimage. For all I recognized the book potential of my Fool's Journey, even while in the midst of it, I was not keen to revisit those times. Once I did, it was not easy to relive the anguish of those ninety-three days and to be reminded of the intensity of a despair that time and events had barely dulled in my memory.

More than once, as I placed myself back on those endless roads and in those lonely hotel rooms, I couldn't help but question the wisdom of my wanderings and, much as I did while experiencing them, second-guess the accuracy of my inner sensings, most notably those related to my visions of Los Angeles and supersonic success.

Many of those questions remained unanswered as I stared at my computer screen, wondering what to say in this Afterword. As much as I tried not to, I repeatedly doubted my intuition, particularly in light of all the ways that COVID-19 trampled on those early Sedona miracles.

The Literate Lizard, for example, is no more. Shuttered first temporarily due to pandemic restrictions, then permanently when the owner fell ill, its closure cut off my primary source of new clients... and revenue. Moving my workshops online made little difference; I couldn't compete with the sudden deluge of Zoom-like offerings. Then, as existing clients completed their work with me and weren't replaced, my income dried up. It was hard not to worry that I was about to repeat my Portland nightmare.

This Afterword was always going to be a part of *Pilgrimage*. And as I worked on the book, I kept hoping that by the time I reached this, its concluding chapter, my circumstances would have shifted enough that I'd be able to write it as a "happily ever after" ending. I wanted to be able to not only recount how my life had turned around after landing here, but how I had overcome the setbacks that wiped out so many of those early gains. I also hoped to have accumulated enough perspective, both on my months of wandering and year of COVID-related reverses, that I could include it in the book's final pages.

Yet, when it came time to write this closing, I was disappointed.

My "happily ever after" was nowhere to be seen, and the deeper meaning of my past and current challenges still eluded me.

"I don't know what to write," I remember muttering. "I don't know where to begin." Then I laughed. That was Toshar's complaint when as an old man he narrates *The MoonQuest*'s Prologue.

The only solution, one I urge in all my workshops and books on writing, was to start. Anywhere. So I did. And as I placed one word after the next, letting the story guide me in my writing much as I had let the road guide me in my journeying, the first glimmerings of awareness shone through the darkness.

The fact is, and it is a fact, not a day has gone by when I haven't been taken care of, even if the means of that care have not always been ones my ego mind would have chosen. Not once have I been abandoned, for all that I feared I would be. That was true through my ninety-three days of wandering, and it has been true through the many scores of days since.

There's a reason this book subtitled itself "A Fool's Journey," and it wasn't merely to mimic the name that attached itself to my travels soon after I left Portland.

"The Way of the Fool is a voyage of faith," I write in *The Way of the Fool: How to Stop Worrying About Life and Start Living It...in 12½ Super-Simple Steps*.

That means trusting in the unknown, the unknowable, the unproven and the unprovable. That means following your heart wherever it leads, however little conventional sense that direction makes. That means knowing that when you step off the cliff in Fool-like fashion, you will always be caught in the arms of whatever you define as God and that you will always be caught before you go splat, even if each succeeding catch scoops you up a few inches closer to the pavement.

When I insist in all my books for writers that "the story knows best," I'm referring not only to the stories we write. I'm making a statement about the stories we live. It can be hard to remember that when we find ourselves in the midst of a challenging chapter, one from which our fearful self would flee if it could. Ironically, it's in those instants, when our trust wavers and our faith is shakiest, that trust and faith are the only qualities guaranteed to see us through.

I was pushed, prodded and pressed to remember that on nearly every one of those ninety-three days, and on more of the days since than I care to admit, including the several it has taken me to compose this Afterword.

What about all those intuitive sensings about LA and the success I felt sure I would achieve there? I confess that as the references to them in my chronicles grew more and more frequent, I grew more and more embarrassed. "I'm going to look like an idiot," I grumbled on more than one occasion, and it took all my creative willpower to not edit some or all of them out.

No, I'm not "living the dream" in Southern California. And yes, the success I experienced when I got to Sedona proved fleeting, at least in worldly terms. Was my vision flawed? Was my intuition wrong?

When I asked those questions, the answers always came back to faith. Could I trust that simply by following the voice of my heart, I *was* living the dream, *my* dream? Could I trust that in living the Fool's Journey, I was successful, on *my* terms, independent of others' definitions? Could I trust that in walking the Way of the Fool, *every* step was the right step? Could I trust that every step got me where I needed to be, even if I could never understand how or why? Could I trust that I *was* home, in my heart, and that that's the only home that, truly, matters?

"Understanding is not required," the main character is reminded several times in *The Bard of Bryn Doon*, echoing identical advice given to a different protagonist in *The SunQuest*, advice that is clearly directed as much at the author as it is to his creations.

Our understanding is limited to our imagination, itself constrained by our knowledge and experience. The heart knows no such boundaries. The heart's journey carries us into worlds beyond that finite imagining and into experiences beyond any we can predict, desire or even pray for, for they reside in the realm of the infinite.

It is into that realm that the Fool's Journey carries us, if we let it...if we surrender into it. If we have the faith to trust that the story — the story of our life — knows best.

"When you let go of that expression of the finite," *The Way of the Fool* continues, "when you leap off the cliff of certainty into the mysteries of the infinite, that's when you fly. That's when you soar."

I did soar through those ninety-three days of pilgrimage, even when it felt as though my belly was grazing the gravel. And I soar still, even when I'm convinced that my wings are broken and that a crash landing is the best I can hope for.

It's impossible not to soar on a Fool's Journey.

Mark David Gerson
October 2021
Sedona, Arizona

The Music of "Pilgrimage"

One of the things that kept me going through those ninety-three days was music. If I was in the car, driving, chances are that Apple Music was streaming from my phone through my car stereo. Along with Kyri, music was often a companion as well on my walks and in my hotel and motel rooms.

Music was also one of the methods my unconscious mind and wisest self used to get my attention through the journey. Particular songs with lyrics relevant to the moment would shuffle onto my phone at significant moments. As well, I'm a light sleeper, and I would often wake up multiple times through the night with snatches of songs playing in my head; sometimes, as with "Defying Gravity," it was the same song each time.

I couldn't possibly list all the songs that inspired, reassured or challenged me through the journey. I can, however, offer a playlist of the tracks mentioned in these chronicles. At this writing, most are available through Apple Music in the US[1] (I'm sure you'll also find many if not all on Spotify, Amazon Music and YouTube Music). Exceptions include the London cast recording of *42nd Street*, sadly no longer available on this side of the Atlantic (I've substituted the original Broadway cast recording) and the Erich Lenk track.

The sole track listed here but not mentioned in the book is "Strength" by Secret Garden, from their *Storyteller* album. I include it because I listened to it whenever I needed reassurance, which was often, both through my final months in Portland and all through my journeying.

---

1. Link to the playlist I created on Apple Music: https://music.apple.com/us/playlist/pilgrimage-a-fools-journey/pl.u-84GvaT3Lzr3

PLAYLIST

1. "Strength" (Secret Garden, *Storyteller*)
2. "Lullaby of Broadway" (*42nd Street*, Original Broadway Cast Recording)
3. "Closure Attunement" (Richard Shulman & Samuel Welsh, *Ascension Harmonics*)
4. "Amazing Grace" (Lari White, *Best of Lari White*)
5. "Home I'll Be" (Rita MacNeil, *Working Man: The Best of Rita MacNeil*)
6. "This Land Is Your Land" (Peter, Paul & Mary, *Around the Campfire*)
7. "All I Ask of You" (*The Phantom of the Opera*, Original Broadway Cast Recording)
8. "This I Promise You" (Shane Filan, *Love Always*)
9. "Let the Wind Blow" (Erich Lenk, *Let the Wind Blow*, single)
10. "When You Wish Upon a Star" (Linda Ronstadt, *For Sentimental Reasons*)
11. "Beautiful in White" (Shane Filan, *Love Always*)
12. "The Impossible Dream" (Il Divo, *A Musical Affair: Live in Japan*)
13. "Getting Out of Town (*42nd Street*, Original Broadway Cast Recording)
14. "How Great Thou Art" (Martina McBride, *Amazing Grace: Music Inspired by the Motion Picture*)
15. "Mi Chamocha" (Amy Sky, *Twilight Rose*)
16. "Don't Rain on My Parade" (Barbra Streisand, *The Essential Barbra Streisand*)
17. "Defying Gravity" (Idina Menzel, *Live: Barefoot at the Symphony*)

18. "Reason to Believe" (Rita MacNeil, *Working Man: The Best of Rita MacNeil*)
19. "Rise Again" (The Rankin Family, *These Are the Moments*)
20. "Happy Days Are Here Again" (Barbra Streisand, *The Essential Barbra Streisand*)
21. "Lucky Day" (Judy Garland, *Great Ladies of Song: Spotlight on Judy Garland*)
22. "God Bless Us Every One (Andrea Bocelli, *Andrea Bocelli: The Complete Pop Albums*)

Gratitude

In classic tarot iconography, the Fool is always represented accompanied by a small dog. On this Fool's Journey, that dog was Kyri. Kyri, a feisty but lovable chihuahua/terrier mix, found me in Portland a few days before my sixty-fourth birthday. It would turn out to be a mutual rescue. Without him to talk to, laugh at, cuddle with and cry to, it would have been harder — perhaps impossible — for me to make it through not only my ninety-three days of journeying but many of the days preceding and following them. It may be unusual for an author to lead off a book's acknowledgments pages with gratitude for his dog, but the journey I have chronicled here was no ordinary one, and Kyri is no ordinary dog. That he settled into it so effortlessly, traveled so easily and supported me so good-naturedly helped me more than I can say. Thank you, Kyri!

Thanks must also go to the two old friends who listened to me so patiently, counseled me so wisely and never tried to talk me out of the journey: Joan Cerio and Sander Dov Freedman.

To the legions of online cheerleaders who sent donations, offered hospitality, shared how my stories from the road inspired them and urged me on in so many other ways, you will never know how much your support helped keep hope alive through those challenging times. I'm forever grateful. I wish I could hug each of you in person or, at the very least, name you all. In the absolute certainty that I would miss some of you, however, I'm reluctant to name any. But you know who you are.

I must also thank those who criticized or challenged me over those weeks and months. Your words were never easy to read or hear. Yet with every one, you forced me to listen to my heart more completely and to trust more fully and Fool-ly. Through them I grew stronger, and that strength helped sustain me when I didn't think I would last another day. You, too, were teachers and guides on the journey. Thank you.

Thanks, too, to Aalia Kazan, who unwittingly helped bring my Pilgrimage to an end, and to Eve Hunter, whose generosity was integral to my support system after I landed. Sadly for all who loved her, Eve left her physical body earlier this year.

In the acknowledgments pages of each of my books, I always thank the spirit and energy of place for its assistance in the writing of it. As with my online supporters, such a list would not only be too long, but I would certainly neglect to mention particular locations. So, to every mile of every road of the fourteen states I passed through, and to every hotel and motel that sheltered me, to every park, field, trail and open space that nurtured me: thank you. And a special shout-out to Sedona, which called me back to it and has supported me through the creation of this book and so much more.

Finally, to my Muse aka my wisest self: Thank you for all the ways you forced me to grow, both through the journey that inspired this book and through the creation of the book itself. *Mahalo nui loa.*

Be Inspired by More of Mark David Gerson's Folly!

The Legend of Q'ntana

"Epic Adventures Rich with Universal Truth!"

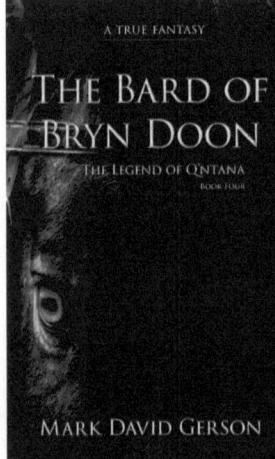
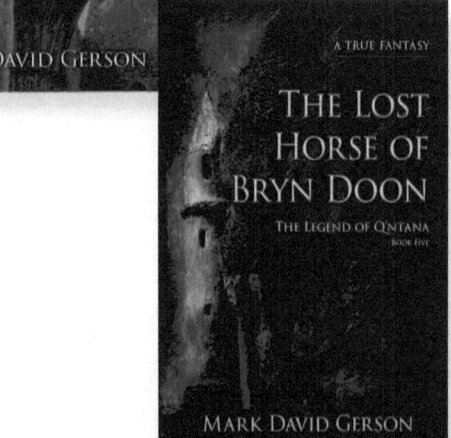

www.ingramcontent.com/pod-product-compliance
Lightning Source LLC
Chambersburg PA
CBHW030146100526
44592CB00009B/147